MAXIMILIEN ROBESPIERRE AND THE FRENCH REVOLUTION

**Elizabeth Schmermund
and Tom McGowen**

Suite 240
New York, NY 10011
USA

enslow.com

Published in 2016 by Enslow Publishing, LLC
101 W. 23rd Street, Suite 240, New York, NY 10011

Copyright © 2016 by Tom McGowen
Enslow Publishing materials copyright © 2016 by Enslow Publishing, LLC.

Library of Congress Cataloging-in-Publication Data
Schmermund, Elizabeth.
 Maximilien Robespierre and the French Revolution / Elizabeth Schmermund and Tom
McGowen.
    pages cm. -- (People and events that changed the world)
 Includes bibliographical references and index.
 Audience: Grade 7 to 8.
 Audience: 12-up.
 ISBN 978-0-7660-7294-7
 1. Robespierre, Maximilien, 1758-1794--Juvenile literature. 2. France--History--Revolution,
1789-1799--Juvenile literature. 3. Revolutionaries--France--Biography--Juvenile literature.
4. France--History--Reign of terror, 1793-1794--Juvenile literature. I. McGowen, Tom. II.
Title.
 DC146.R6S34 2016
 944.04'1092--dc23
                        2015029190

Printed in the United States of America

To Our Readers: We have done our best to make sure all website addresses in this book
were active and appropriate when we went to press. However, the author and the publisher
have no control over and assume no liability for the material available on those websites
or on any websites they may link to. Any comments or suggestions can be sent by e-mail to
customerservice@enslow.com.

Portions of this book originally appeared in the book *Robespierre and the French
Revolution in World History.*

Photo Credits: Throughout book: EduardSV/Shutterstock.com (chapter head texture);
cover, p. 1 Jean Victor Schnetz/Getty Images (Fighting at the Hotel de Ville), Angelus/
Wikimedia Commons/the french tricolor cockade/Documentation License (French flag on
spine); p. 4 Mike H/Shutterstock.com; pp. 10, 79 Buyenlarge/Archive Photos/Getty Images; p.
13 Ann Ronan Pictures/Print Collector/Archive Photos/Getty Images; p. 17 Georgios Kollidas/
Shutterstock.com; pp. 19, 44, 82, 97 Hulton Archive/Getty Images; pp. 22, 28 DeAgostini/Getty
Images; p. 26 Brian Kinney/Shutterstock.com; p. 32 Hulton Fine Art Collection/DeAgostini/
Getty Images; p. 36 The Print Collector/Print Collector/Hulton Archive/Getty Images; pp. 40,
86 Bob Thomas/Popperfoto/Getty Images; p. 47 Marzolino/Shutterstock.com; p. 53 lynea/
Shutterstock.com; p. 57 Fotosearch/Archive Photos/Getty Images; p. 59 iStock.com/Roberto
A. Sanchez; p. 62 Hulton Archive/Hulton Royals Collection/Getty Images; p. 66 Imagno/
Hulton Fine Art Collection/Getty Images; pp. 70, 106 Universal History Archive/UIG via Getty
Images; p. 73 Apic/Hulton Archive/Getty Images; p. 93 Photo12/UIG via Getty Images; p. 101
Keystone-France/Gamma-Keystone via Getty Images; p. 111 SeM/UIG via Getty Images; p.
112 Library of Congress, Prints and Photographs Division; p. 117 JOEL ROBINE/AFP/Getty
Images.

CONTENTS

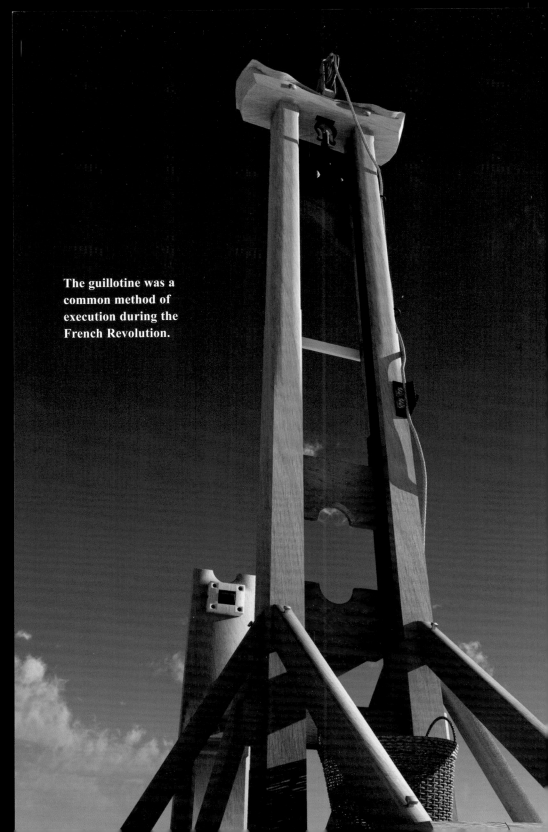

The guillotine was a common method of execution during the French Revolution.

The Guillotine

Thousands of people packed the square in the middle of the city. It was a special day and a crowd had gathered to get a good look at what was going to happen. Some people had seen this before while, for others, this was their first time. Celebrations and special events were often held in this square, too. But today the people were here to see blood.

At the center of the square was a high wooden platform with steps leading up to it. On the platform was a machine for killing people. This machine, called a guillotine, was made up of two tall wooden posts with a heavy blade suspended high between them. A thick cord held the blade in place. The victim would be placed facedown with his or her head between the posts. When the cord was cut, the blade would be released and come sliding swiftly down with enough force to slice through the victim's neck.

On this day, on the platform beside the guillotine were several men. These were the executioners—the men who would use the guillotine to cut off the heads of those who had been sentenced to die on this day. The crowd was gathered in the square to watch the execution.

All around the square platform were arranged several rows of chairs and benches. Seated on these were women of all ages. They were in the best place to see everything that would happen up on the platform. Most of the women had balls of yarn in their laps and knitting needles in their hands and were industriously knitting. They talked and laughed as they worked.

The sudden roar of a cheer erupted from the crowd. At one end of the square, a vehicle was emerging from between two buildings. It was a two-wheeled wooden cart, painted red, drawn by a pair of plodding horses. Standing in the cart, behind the driver, were several people, both men and women. Their hands were tied behind their backs.

The crowd parted for the cart, and the horses clip-clopped their way toward the center of the square. The driver brought them to a halt beside the platform. Two of the executioners came down and roughly helped one of the prisoners, a man, out of the cart. Quickly, one of the executioners cut the man's hair short, so it would not get in the way of the guillotine's blade. Then, they led him up the steps, onto the platform.

The man was pushed down to lie flat on a wooden plank and was strapped into place so he could not move. The plank was shoved forward so that the man's head went into a wooden brace that positioned his neck directly beneath the blade. His head stuck out over a basket that sat on the platform.

One of the executioners cut the cord. The blade hurtled down.

Blood sprayed out over the women in the front row, falling on the objects they were knitting. The women laughed with glee. They were knitting stockings for soldiers who were fighting for the country in foreign lands, and they believed the spots of blood would make the men fight harder.

An executioner reached down into the basket. He lifted up the severed head, blood still dripping from the neck, and held it up for the crowd to see. There was a roar of approval from the people who had watched the execution. They cheered and applauded.

What could cause such a horrible spectacle as this? What could cause ordinary people to turn into savages, rejoicing at the sight of the bloody death of other people?

What caused it was an event that took place more than two hundred years ago in the nation of France. That event is known as the French Revolution. It became a bloody and terrible spectacle. But it began very quietly, in the year 1789.

Primary Source:
From the Recollections of
John Gideon Millingen,
1790–1801

The process of execution was also a sad and heart-rending spectacle . . . On one side of the scaffold were drawn out a sufficient number of carts, with large baskets painted red, to receive the heads and bodies of the victims. Those bearing the condemned moved on slowly to the foot of the guillotine . . . Most of these unfortunates ascended the scaffold with a determined step—many of them looked up firmly on the menacing instrument of death, beholding for the last time the rays of the glorious sun, beaming on the polished axe; and I have seen some young men actually dance a few steps before they went up to be strapped to the perpendicular plane, which was then tilted to a horizontal plane in a moment, and ran on the grooves until the neck was secured and closed in by a moving board, when the head passed through what was called in derision, *la lunette republicaine* [the republican telescope]; the weighty knife was then dropped with a heavy fall; and, with incredible dexterity and rapidity, two executioners tossed the body into the basket, while another threw the head after it.[1]

L'Ancien Régime

In 1789 France was one of the most powerful nations in the world. It had recently made use of its powerful army and navy to help the American colonies win their war for independence from Great Britain. It had a powerful king, famous and influential politicians, writers, and artists, and colonies all over the world. French was the language of the rich and the educated and was spoken in many countries. But France was also in financial trouble. Because of its many wars—including helping the Americans during their revolution—the country owed a lot of money.

In the *Ancien Régime* (France's government before the revolution), feudalism, the system of lords and subjects, was in use since medieval times. The lords—the king, the nobles, and the high officials of the Catholic Church—had total power over the subjects, the common people. There was no freedom of speech, no freedom of religion, no freedom of the press, and very few freedoms of any other kind.

The Estate System

The people of France were divided into three classes, or estates. The First Estate was the clergy, or religious workers,

Priests and other clergy members were a small but influential group within the estate system in eighteenth-century France.

making up about one percent of the total population. The French clergy was almost entirely made up of priests and nuns of the Roman Catholic Church. By law, this was the official religion of France. Protestants and Jews were not permitted to worship openly, and there were no other religions in the country.

The Second Estate was the nobility, people who had titles before their name—duke and duchess, count and countess, marquis and marquess. The nobility was composed of some thirty thousand families, about two hundred thousand people. Supposedly, they were descended from warriors who had helped the first king conquer France in ancient times, or from persons who had helped other kings in some way and had been rewarded with wealth, land, and privileges. So, nobles owned much of the land of France. Noblemen commanded the regiments and armies and fleets of the French Army and Navy and were the king's counselors and government officials. They also held most of the positions of highest authority in the Church, because they were appointed to such positions by the king. However, not all nobles were wealthy. Some owned nothing more than a small farm and did much of their own farmwork.

The Third Estate was the commoners, some twenty-six million strong. There were basically two groups of commoners. One group, known in France as the *bourgeoisie*, was what might be called the middle class in America. They were owners of large farms or large or small businesses, shop owners, doctors, lawyers, and judges. These people were generally prosperous, and some were as wealthy as nobles. The other group was the laborers. Many of these were factory workers, dock workers, wagon drivers, grave diggers, or servants who worked for nobles. But most—

about twenty-one million—were peasants, farmers who owned only tiny farms or who lived and worked on farms belonging to nobles or to the Church. Many laborers, especially the peasants, were desperately, agonizingly poor. An Englishman who had traveled through France wrote of seeing many peasants who looked more like skinny scarecrows than human beings. Another English traveler told of ragged, hungry-looking children who made his heart ache.

Feudalism and Injustice

But poor or not, nearly all commoners were subject to a great many taxes, payments, and obligations. They had to pay a yearly flat-rate tax (the same amount for everyone) to the government, as well as a kind of income tax consisting of an amount equal to one twentieth of their income. They also had to pay a tithe, equal to the value of one tenth of their income and all their belongings, to the Church. They paid taxes on all the salt, wine, tobacco, soap, leather, and ironware they bought. If they happened to live on land that belonged to the Church, they paid a tax on that. If they lived on a noble's land, they paid him rent.

Living on a noble's land also meant many additional costs and restrictions. In order to grind any grain they raised into flour, or to press grapes into juice for wine, peasants had to pay a nobleman for the use of his flour mill or winepress. In many places, if there were a bridge crossing a stream on the noble's land, the peasants had to pay a fee for using the bridge. They were responsible for the upkeep and maintenance of all the roads on the land, at their own expense, and this often took them away from their farms— where their efforts were needed to plant or harvest crops

Under the system of feudalism, peasants worked the land while the landowners reaped the benefits.

Primary Source: An Englishman named Arthur Young Writing About France, 1787–1789

. . . The abuses attending the levy of taxes were heavy and universal . . . [W]hat must have been the state of the poor people paying heavy taxes, from which the nobility and clergy were exempted? A cruel aggravation of their misery, to see those who could best afford to pay, exempted because able! . . . The *corvees* [a tax in kind; it was paid through labor service rather than in money], or police of the roads, were annually the ruin of many hundreds of farmers. . . .[1]

that meant their livelihood—for weeks at a time. Worst of all, they were forbidden to hunt or trap any animals on the land. This not only kept them from a valuable food supply, but also meant a loss of some of their crops, because animals and birds ate many of the seeds peasants planted, and then ate much of the plants that grew from the seeds that were left. But a peasant caught trying to prevent this by killing an animal or bird could be shot and killed by the noble's gamekeepers.

Most of the lower ranks of the clergy—parish priests, monsigneurs, and abbots—had come from commoner families and thought of themselves as equal with commoners. But to most nobles, the commoners were far beneath them. Their contemptuous term for commoners was *canaille*, meaning "vulgar," or low and crude.

A Hope for Change

The nobles and the high officials of the Church were completely free from having to pay most taxes. Thus, the commoners were literally paying the living expenses of the nobles and high Church officials. While a commoner might have to struggle to make enough to feed, dress, and house his family, many nobles were spending millions for nothing more than lavish parties and entertainments. And so, there was bitter resentment among most members of the Third Estate toward the nobles.

There was resentment even among the wealthier people of the Third Estate, the bourgeoisie, especially those who had created large, profitable businesses and industries. Despite their valuable contributions to the economy of France, they were given no more rights than the poorest peasant. They could not dream of ever becoming high-ranking military or naval commanders, officials of the Church, or counselors of the king. Such things were forbidden to them. Like the peasants, they were just *canaille*.

Adding to all this resentment was a flood of new ideas sweeping through France among the educated members of the Third Estate, as well as some nobles and priests. These ideas, known collectively as the Enlightenment—which meant an opening up of the mind—had been growing for years. Since the 1600s, philosophers throughout Europe, such as Frenchmen Voltaire and Montesquieu, and the Swiss philosopher Jean-Jacques Rousseau, had been writing that the governments and ways of life of nations should be based on logical thinking and science, rather than on old traditions and customs. For these men, such things as kings and nobles and established religions simply were not logical. They argued that all people should be equal and that governments should be based on the needs of all the people, rather than just a privileged few.

Many members of the bourgeoisie saw these new ideas as a way to a better life, and believed France should have a new kind of government. They also wanted more rights for the Third Estate and less for the king, nobles, and Church. Many of them wanted a constitution for France, like the constitution of Great Britain, which provided equal power for king, nobles, and commoners. A few wanted a constitution like that of the United States, with no king, no nobles, and a government controlled by the people. Of course, the king, most of the nobles, and Church officials of France were bitterly opposed to such ideas.

Poverty and Desperation

In addition to the simmering resentment over inequality, there was also concern throughout the Third Estate over the growing difficulty of making a living. France had been involved in a number of wars during the last fifty years. This had cost enormous amounts of money. As a result, the French treasury was nearly empty, and the government had to cut back on many of the things it regularly bought. This hurt business and caused many people to lose their jobs. To make things worse, there had been bad harvests throughout the country, so there was a shortage of grain. Bread, the main food of the poor—for some, their only food—was becoming scarce. It had nearly doubled in price. For years, a family-size four-pound loaf of bread had cost eight sous—

around two dollars. Now the price was up to three and even four dollars a loaf. Thus, a farmworker who made only five sous a day, about $1.25, could buy a loaf of bread only every three days. Trying to live for three days on one day's worth of food literally meant starvation for him and his family. Many people could not survive, and hordes of beggars—men, women, and children—began to appear.

Jean-Jacques Rousseau was a writer and philosopher who believed that people needed to break away from old traditions like the class system in France.

Some people became desperate. They began to disobey laws and turn to violence. Throughout the countryside, French peasants banded together. Ignoring the laws that prohibited them from hunting, they began to hunt and trap rabbits, deer, pheasants, and other creatures that by law "belonged" only to the nobles. In some places, when game wardens working for nobles tried to prevent the hunting and trapping, they were simply murdered.

In many farm areas, bands of hungry people, mainly women determined to see that their families were fed, began to make raids on barges and wagon trains that were bringing grain into the cities. They took what they felt they needed.

In the cities, too, desperate and starving people became violent. In the city of Marseilles, the town hall was stormed

Primary Source: Jean Jacques Rousseau's *Social Contract*, 1762

Man is born free, and yet is everywhere in fetters [chains]. He is governed, obliged to obey laws. What is it that legitimises this subjection to government? I think I can solve the problem.

The problem with which men are confronted in these circumstances may be put thus: "To find a form of association that defends and protects, with all the common force, the person and property of each partner, and by which each partner, uniting himself with all the rest, nevertheless obeys only himself, and remains as free as heretofore."

To this problem the social contract affords a solution. The essence of the pact is the total and unreserved alienation by each partner of all his rights to the community as a whole. No individual can retain any rights that are not possessed equally by all other individuals without the compact being thereby violated . . . .[2]

French peasants, despite working from morning until night, had little to show for their efforts. By the late 1700s, these commoners were starting to get fed up.

and looted. In Aix-en-Provence, there was a riot. Soldiers called to stop it fired into the crowd, killing several people. In Paris, a rumor began that the wealthy owner of a large, prosperous wallpaper factory had said that wages for workers were too high. A huge crowd of thousands of angry jobless people marched to the factory, chanting, "Death to the rich, death to the aristocrats!"[3] They poured into the factory and set it on fire; then went on to the owner's nearby house and looted and destroyed that. Soldiers appeared. Here, too, they fired into the crowd. Some six hundred people were killed or wounded.

Thus, as the year 1789 slipped into spring, there was resentment, anger, fear, and violence spreading throughout the French nation. Everyone felt that something had to be done, soon, to make things better. Their one great hope lay in an event that was going to happen in May of that year in a little town called Versailles, where there was a splendid royal palace. There was going to be a great meeting held there. Men representing each of the three estates were going to get together to try to solve France's troubles. And so, as the trees began to sprout buds and the air began to grow warm, the eyes and thoughts of all France were on Versailles.

One of the people who had Versailles uppermost in his mind was a thirty-year-old lawyer living in the northern town of Arras. He had been selected to go to Versailles as one of the representatives of the Third Estate. His name was Maximilien François Marie Isadore de Robespierre.

Revolutionary Rumblings

Louis XVI, also known as Louis Auguste de France, the king of France, was timid, indecisive, and more interested in sports than in being a monarch. He grew up in the shadow of his older brother, Louis Duc de Bourgogne, who died at the age of nine. In 1789 Louis XVI was thirty-five years old and had four young children. He was chubby and tended to eat and drink too much. Louis wanted to be a good king, but he lacked self-confidence and did not make decisions that could help lead his country out of debt. But Louis XVI tried to do his best and allowed his subjects to freely practice their religion. He was well liked by most of the French people.

This was not true of his queen, however. Her name was Marie Antoinette, and she was not a French woman. She was an Austrian, the sister of the emperor of the Austrian-Hungarian Empire. She had been reared as a princess with every luxury and had become rather vain and self-centered. She spent enormous amounts of money on clothes, cosmetics, and hairstyles. She also spent a great amount of time and money trying to keep herself amused. She was able to talk

King Louis XVI became King of France in 1774. His reign was marked by grave financial difficulties and social unrest.

the king into doing just about anything she wanted him to do.

The king had two younger brothers: the Comte (Count) d'Artois and the Comte de Provence. He also had two sisters—Clotilde, who was married to the king of Sardinia, and Elizabeth. Louis paid for nearly everything Elizabeth and his brothers did, including gambling debts. He also listened to their advice, which usually was not very good. Marie Antoinette and the Comte d'Artois often teamed up to convince Louis what he ought to do.

Louis was very much concerned about the problems of his nation in 1789, particularly the lack of money. But he was the sort of person who, when confronted with a problem, simply ignored it, apparently hoping it would just go away. He left most decisions to his counselors.

One of his major counselors was the minister of finance, the person who was responsible for seeing that France had enough money. Louis's minister of finance was a Swiss man by the name of Jacques Necker. Necker had been a banker in Switzerland. He understood a great deal about how to raise money and invest it to make it grow. However, Switzerland was a republic, with no king or nobles, so Necker was a commoner. The French nobles, including the queen and the king's two brothers, did not like him. He had once published a report that showed how much of the tax money spent in France went to support the nobles, and one of his main ideas for raising money to refill the French treasury was to tax the nobles and the clergy. Of course, the nobles were completely against this. They let it be known that they would refuse to accept such a change in their way of life. However, the Third Estate felt that Necker was on their side and looked on him as a friend.

The Three Estates Meet

To help solve France's problems, Necker and some of the king's other counselors advised Louis to call a great meeting to which elected representatives of each of the three estates could come to offer their ideas. Such meetings had been called before, by past kings, and were known as Estates-General. So, in the summer of 1788, Louis had ordered the members of the three estates in each region of France to hold elections and select delegates to represent them at the Estates-General, to be held in 1789. He also ordered the members of each estate to draw up lists of grievances, or complaints, about matters affecting them that seemed unfair or unjust.

To most members of the Third Estate, this looked like an answer to their prayers. Not only was the king going to try to solve the problems of food and money, but he was also apparently going to do something about all the injustices they were suffering from taxes and the special privileges of the First and Second Estates. People of every region began to list their protests, and these turned out to be much alike everywhere. They wanted taxes made the same for everyone, with the nobles and clergy paying taxes as commoners did. They wanted freedom of the press, with no more censorship of books, newspapers, or magazines. They wanted greater religious freedom, at least for Protestants. There were many demands for more freedom, for more equality, and for a constitution for France.

In late April, the delegates began to arrive in the town of Versailles. The representatives of the Third Estate consisted of 178 merchants and shopkeepers, 158 judges of low courts, and 214 lawyers. One of these was Maximilien de

Robespierre, delegate from the region of Artois, in the far north of France.

Two Delegates

Maximilien de Robespierre was born in 1758, the first child of a well-to-do family. His father was a lawyer. By the time Maximilien was six, he had a brother and two sisters, but it was then that his mother died. Soon after, his father abandoned the four children to relatives and left town. From then on, Maximilien was reared by two aunts.

When he was eleven, he won a scholarship to one of the best schools in France, located in Paris. He lived at the school for the next twelve years and was regarded as a brilliant student. After graduating, he became a lawyer and returned to his town of Arras, where he lived with his brother and sisters.

Maximilien was small and slim, with a high, wide forehead; a long, thin nose; and watery, red-rimmed eyes. In Versailles, he dressed very carefully, in a worn black suit, and his hair was always perfectly arranged and powdered, which was then the style. None of the other delegates knew much about him, but in Arras, he was known as a staunch defender of the poor. He had been the lawyer for many poor people, trying to gain justice for them and prevent them from being treated unfairly. As the other delegates got to know him, they learned that de Robespierre admired the great philosopher Rousseau tremendously. Like Rousseau, he was a fiercely intense believer in democracy, or government of the people.

Another of the delegates was a forty-year-old man who was well-known to everyone. He was the Comte de Mirabeau, a strange-looking person with a bulky body and huge head

Versailles is the royal palace just outside of Paris that was the residence of King Louis XVI when the French Revolution began.

and neck. As a child, he had suffered from the disease known as smallpox, which covered a person's body with blisters that generally left scars, and Mirabeau's big face was pitted and pocked with such scars. His great-great-grandfather had been a commoner who was made a noble by a past king, so Mirabeau was technically a nobleman. However, most nobles whose families went back many hundreds of years looked down on such people, and Mirabeau had often been treated with contempt. So although he believed in monarchy, rule by a king, Mirabeau hated the nobility and had come to the Estates-General as a delegate of the Third Estate. He was known as a powerful speaker, who could excite people with his voice and words. He also had a reputation as a wild, partying sort of person.

The Third Estate is Stifled

The meeting of the Estates-General was to begin on May 5, 1789. But even before the meeting started, it quickly began to look as if attempts were going to be made to keep the delegates of the Third Estate "in their place." All of them had been instructed to wear only black clothes, the traditional garb of the low class. When they went to meet the king in the great palace of Versailles, they were allowed to enter only through side doors. Instead of meeting with all the delegates at once, the king met first with the delegates of the First Estate and then with the nobles of the Second Estate, in his own private rooms. Then, after making the Third Estate delegates wait a long time, the king met with them in another room. He did not speak to any of them except for one elderly man. Most of them felt slighted.

More slights were to come. The next day, when all the delegates went to church for a special mass, the First and Second Estate delegates all had reserved seats, but the Third Estate delegates were left to find their own places. In the parade of delegates that marched through the streets of Versailles, the men of the Third Estate were put at the front, which actually meant that they were considered of least importance.

The meeting of the Estates-General was held in the large hall of a building that generally was used as a theater where plays were performed. The meeting began with a short speech by the king. He did not mention any of the issues the Third Estate delegates were most concerned about, such as more rights for the commoners and a reduction of taxes. He seemed concerned only with raising money for the French treasury. Then there was a long, dry, droning speech by Necker, finished by one of his secretaries, which was also

A portrait
of a young
Robespierre.

about raising money. It began to seem to the Third Estate delegates as if no attention at all were going to be paid to the wishes and ideas of the common people.

The next day, the delegates of the three estates were split up into three rooms. The meeting was arranged so that the delegates of each estate, after discussing matters among themselves and coming to an agreement, would cast a single vote representing their decision. Thus, each estate had one vote. What this meant, of course, was that the First and Second Estates would be able to outvote the Third Estate, two to one. Thus, the delegates representing only about 4 percent of France would have more power than the delegates representing 96 percent! The Third Estate would never have a chance to make any of the changes it was hoping for.

Primary Source: Article from the Third Estate of Versailles, 1789

Art. 70. We demand, for the benefit of commerce, the abolition of all exclusive privileges:
- The removal of customs barriers to the frontiers;
- The most complete freedom in trade;
- The revision and reform of all laws relative to commerce;
- Encouragement for all kinds of manufacture, viz.: premiums, bounties and advances;
- Rewards to artisans and laborers for useful inventions.[1]

The National Assembly

The Third Estate could not agree to this. Their wish was that the delegates of the three estates should all meet together, and that every delegate of each estate should have one vote. The problems facing the nation could be discussed, debated, and voted on, with the majority vote winning. In other words, they wanted a *democratic* way of voting. That way, the Third Estate delegates, with the help of votes from members of the First and Second Estates who agreed with them, might be able to gain some of the changes they wanted.

There were delegates of the First and Second Estates who were willing to side with the Third Estate. Among the First Estate delegates were many ordinary priests who wanted to help reduce the taxes and restrictions on the desperately poor peasants and who bitterly detested the noble bishops, archbishops, and cardinals, who possessed enormous wealth. There were clear-thinking noblemen who realized that the situation in France had to be changed, or the country would simply come apart. One of these was the Marquis de Lafayette, who had fought on the American side in the American Revolution and was regarded as a hero in both the United States and France. It was Lafayette who first suggested the idea of holding a meeting of the Estates-General.

But the high officials of the Church and the majority of nobles of the Second Estate were well aware that they could lose their power if the method of voting was changed. They utterly refused to accept any change.

Days went by. Nothing happened and nothing was accomplished. Then, both de Robespierre, who was now calling himself Robespierre, and Mirabeau suggested that the clergymen be invited to join with the Third Estate delegates in an effort to make some progress. The invitation was made.

This caused a tumult among the delegates of the First Estate. Many priests wanted to join the Third Estate delegates, but the noble archbishops, bishops, and cardinals refused to consider such an idea.

However, the delegates of the Third Estate had come to the Estates-General specifically to present the wishes and demands of the commoners to the king, and that was what they intended to do. For days, they talked matters over among themselves. One of the delegates, a clergyman named Sieyès, pointed out that the Third Estate represented more than 96 percent of the French population, which was basically the entire French nation. Therefore, the Third Estate delegates could claim that only they actually represented the nation. Another delegate suggested they should give themselves the name of National Assembly, to show this. This was voted on, and the name was accepted by 491 votes. The delegates then started to work on the creation of new laws and decrees for things the commoners wanted.

The Tennis Court Oath

On June 19, the majority of priest-delegates of the First Estate voted to join the National Assembly. This meant that power was now in the hands of the Third Estate. A cardinal and archbishop of the First Estate and several noblemen of the Second Estate rushed to see the king. Desperately, they urged him to halt the entire meeting of the Estates-General and bring it to an end.

The king did not know what to do. Necker suggested that he agree to many of the things the Third Estate wanted, which would make him tremendously popular with the

The Tennis Court Oath was signed by almost all members of the National Assembly after they were locked out of the meeting of the Estates-General.

commoners. But the queen and the king's two brothers argued that Louis could not give in to the commoners. They insisted that he had to show his power and do something to keep the Third Estate delegates in their place.

Thus, on the morning of June 20, when the members of the National Assembly went to begin their meeting, they found the room locked and under guard. They were told that it was being made ready for a special meeting the king intended to hold and could not be used until then. This not only prevented them from meeting, but also kept the clergymen from officially joining them. They felt sure this was really just the first step in an attempt to break them up and force them to leave Versailles.

They determined to strike back. In a drizzling rain, they all walked through the streets of Versailles until they found a building large enough to hold them, which was an indoor tennis court, and took it over for their meeting. All but one of the delegates swore an oath—known as the Tennis Court Oath—that they would not separate from one another until the king and nobles of the Second Estate agreed to accept a constitution for France.

They were deliberately defying the king. The French Revolution was under way.

Primary Source Document: Tennis Court Oath, 1789

This proposal is approved by unanimous applause. The Assembly quickly decrees the following:

The National Assembly, considering that it has been called to establish the constitution of the realm, to bring about the regeneration of public order, and to maintain the true principles of monarchy; nothing may prevent it from continuing its deliberations in any place it is forced to establish itself.

Finally, the National Assembly exists wherever its members are gathered. [It] decrees that all members of this assembly immediately take a solemn oath never to separate, and to reassemble wherever circumstances require, until the constitution of the realm is established and fixed upon solid foundations; and that said oath having been sworn, all members and each one individually confirm this unwavering resolution with his signature.[2]

The Storming of the Bastille

The Tennis Court Oath showed France that the National Assembly refused to back down from their stated goals. Hearing about the Oath, more than one hundred fifty clergymen, who were delegates of the First Estate, decided to join the National Assembly. Many nobles, realizing the strength and dedication of the National Assembly, also joined the commoners with the sincere hope of change. This was a turning point in the Third Estate's fight for equal rights.

On June 23, 1789, when the special meeting called by the king was held, the building where it took place was surrounded by soldiers. The king made a short speech in which he agreed to a few changes the Third Estate had asked for, such as no new taxes and greater freedom of the press. But he did not mention equality for the Third Estate, an end to privileges for the nobility, or a constitution. To end his speech, he announced that nothing would be done without his approval, and he ordered the three groups of delegates to leave and to go back to work the next day in their three separate rooms. In other words, he was commanding all the commoners, clergymen, and nobles who now formed the

The 1789 meetings of the Estates-General were held in a heavily guarded room at Versailles.

National Assembly, to break up and return to their original three delegations. He was refusing to recognize that a National Assembly even existed, and he had made it plain that most of the changes the commoners were hoping for were not going to be made.

Despite the king's command to leave, the members of the National Assembly remained in the hall. The nobleman who had been acting as master of ceremonies reminded them in a loud voice that they had been ordered to go. It was later said by a number of delegates that Mirabeau then stood up, and in an even louder voice, told the man, "we are here by the will of the people and we . . . will not be dispersed except at the point of bayonets!"[1]

Outside, the building was now ringed by a throng of thousands of common people. They had come from Paris, which was only twelve miles away. Fearing a riot, the officer in command of the soldiers sent to keep peace ordered them to fire into the people, to inspire terror and make the crowd break up. Just a few months earlier, before the Estates-General began, the soldiers would have obeyed. But now they knew about what the National Assembly was trying to do for commoners, and they were all commoners themselves. They refused to fire on their own people.

The king was informed that the National Assembly had ignored his command to leave the hall. "Very well, let them stay," he growled, as if he did not really care.[2] But when he learned that French soldiers were refusing to obey their officers, he grew concerned. This meant he could no longer depend on those troops. On the advice of some of his counselors, he ordered some of the army's regiments of foreign soldiers to come to Paris. These soldiers, mostly Swiss and Germans, would not refuse to fire on French commoners if ordered to do so. They could be used to make the National Assembly obey, and to break up the rowdy crowds of Paris.

Camille Desmoulin's Call

In 1789 Paris was a community of half a million people. It was then, as it still is, the main city of France. As July began, the streets of Paris became filled with surging, restless crowds of thousands of commoners. Many of them were out of work and starving. They were joined by many soldiers who were no longer willing to serve the king. These men walked about in groups, shouting such things as "Long live the Third Estate! We belong to it and will never fight, except in its defense!"[3]

Suddenly, on July 11, the king fired Necker and ordered him to leave France. He was replaced by the Baron de Breteuil, a nobleman who was known to be in favor of leaving taxes the way they were. The crowds in Paris swelled. Their mood was now ugly. A man who was their friend had been swept away and replaced by an enemy. The people felt betrayed.

In the heart of Paris was a large building known as the Royal Palace. Part of it actually was a palace, belonging to the Duke of Orleans, but much of it held shops and cafés. There was a park-like garden in the center, and people would stroll through it and visit the shops. On the afternoon of July 12, crowds were surging through the garden, seeking news. Everyone knew that King Louis had sent for foreign soldiers, and the people of Paris were fearfully expecting to be attacked.

A young man named Camille Desmoulins was standing in front of one of the cafés with some friends. He was a part-time lawyer in his twenties who had run for election as a delegate to the Estates-General but had not been selected. Desmoulins and his friends were discussing the rumors swirling through the city. Suddenly, Desmoulins could not contain himself. He leaped up onto a café table and began to speak to the crowd flowing by.

Desmoulins announced that he was calling on the people of Paris to take up weapons and fight! The German troops the king has sent for are here, he declared, and they will come into Paris tonight to butcher everyone![4] He tugged a leaf off a tree branch by his head and stuck it in his hat, urging everyone to "—take a green cockade, the color of hope—," as a symbol of their common cause.[5] Then he yanked a pistol from his pocket and brandished it in the air. "I would die rather than submit to servitude!" he yelled defiantly.[6]

Desmoulins's fiery speech roused the crowd to a peak of excitement. He was cheered and hailed as a hero. People began seizing every green thing they could find and fastening it to themselves. They streamed away in all directions to spread the word of Desmoulins's speech and to search for weapons. Later in the afternoon, as Desmoulins had said would happen, there was an attack by foreign troops. A regiment of German cavalry charged into a crowd, killing an elderly man and wounding several other people.

The Citizens Arm Themselves

On the morning of July 13, the clanging of hundreds of church bells awoke Parisians as a warning of danger in the streets. Mobs were roving everywhere, searching for weapons with which to defend themselves. Some found swords and pikes, long spears that had been used by soldiers a hundred years earlier. Others broke into gunmakers' shops and helped themselves to muskets and pistols.

But swords, pikes, and a few firearms would not be enough to defend against thousands of well-armed soldiers. A fighting force was needed, not only to defend the city but to preserve order. In every part of the city, units of volunteer militia were formed—ordinary citizens willing to fight as soldiers to protect their families and neighbors. They had no uniforms, but to identify themselves they pinned circles of red and blue ribbon, the colors of the city of Paris, to their hats or coat lapels. They needed a commander, and the obvious choice was the Marquis de Lafayette. He accepted several days later, and gave these citizen soldiers the name of National Guard.

Revolutionary Camille Desmoulins gave a spontaneous speech in June of 1789 that made him an instant hero to many Parisians.

Primary Source: Letter from Camille Desmoulins, July 1789

Dearest father,

I can now write to you . . . How things have changed over the last three days! Last Sunday, Paris was dismayed at the dismissal of M. Necker. Although I was getting people worked up, no one would take up arms. About three o'clock I went to the Palais-Royal. I was deploring our lack of courage to a group of people when three young men came by, holding hands and shouting *Aux armes*! (To arms!) I joined them and since my enthusiasm was quite obvious, I was surrounded and pressed to climb up on a table. Immediately six thousand people gathered around me. . . .

I was choking from the hundreds of ideas that overwhelmed me and, my thoughts a jumble, I spoke: "To arms!" I cried, "To arms! Let us all wear green cockades, the color of hope." . . . I grabbed a green ribbon and was the first to pin it to my hat. My action spread like wildfire! The noise from the tumult reached the camp . . . Prince Lambesc, leading the regiment of Royal-Allemands [part of the French Royal army], entered the Tuileries on horseback. He personally cut down an unarmed French guardsman with his sword, and knocked over women and children. The crowd became furious, and from that point on, there was but a single cry heard across Paris: To Arms![7]

Word spread that there were thirty-two thousand muskets in the military hospital for veterans, the Invalides. Early on the morning of July 14, an immense crowd of thousands stormed the hospital and seized the muskets and a number of cannons.

However, to fire these weapons, gunpowder was needed. A musket had to have a quantity of gunpowder shoved down into the barrel, and a bullet pushed down on top of that. Someone remembered that 250 barrels of gunpowder, about 30,000 pounds, were stored at a place well-known to Parisians—the Bastille. The crowd swarmed toward it.

The Bastille was a fortress built in the 1300s and later turned into a prison. It was a huge, gloomy gray building with eight ninety-foot towers, encircled by a deep ditch that had once been a moat. For centuries, it had been a symbol of the tyranny of France's rulers. It was the object of dreadful stories of innocent people condemned to lifelong imprisonment in horrible dungeons and subjected to brutal tortures. Rumors said it was filled with prisoners, but in July 1789, there were actually only seven. Four were convicted criminals, one was an attempted murderer, and two were mentally disturbed. The Bastille's guard consisted of eighty-two crippled army veterans and thirty-two soldiers of a Swiss regiment. But the crowd that arrived at the Bastille could see that there were cannons pointing at the street from all the towers.

The man in charge of the Bastille, the Marquis de Launay, was an elderly nobleman who simply did not know what to do when the gigantic crowd appeared and demanded that the store of gunpowder be turned over to them. He decided to stall for time, hoping that troops would show up to disperse the crowd. He offered to negotiate.

Victory at the Bastille

A delegation of men selected by the crowd entered the Bastille to talk to de Launay. It was now ten o'clock, and he invited the men to have a late breakfast with him. De Launay seemed ready to consent to the crowd's demands and even agreed to pull the cannons on the towers back so that they could not fire. But as time dragged on, the people outside became convinced that the men they had sent in had been taken prisoner.

The mob surged forward and broke into the building's inner courtyard. Blasts of cannonfire from the towers killed eighty-three and wounded eighty-eight. Then, soldiers accompanying the crowd pushed up cannons and aimed them at the main gate. De Launay decided he had better surrender. The gate was unlocked and the drawbridge lowered. The crowd rushed into the Bastille.

In the wild scuffle that followed, six of de Launay's men were killed. Two of the men in the crowd seized de Launay and tried to get him safely away, but another man wildly attacked him. Trying to defend himself, de Launay kicked the man, who shrieked in pain. An enraged man stabbed de Launay in the stomach with a bayonet. He fell writhing to the ground, and instantly, other members of the crowd began stabbing him with swords and bayonets and firing pistols and muskets into his body until he was dead. The man he had kicked, an unemployed cook, cut off de Launay's head with a knife, and it was stuck on the point of a pike. Holding the dripping head high, the crowd surged off in triumph. The revolution had now turned bloody. As time went on, much more blood would be spilled.

In the weeks following the storming of the Bastille, the great fortress was gradually torn down. The people of Paris

On July 14, 1789, the French people stormed the Bastille. The bloody event marked the official beginning of the Revolution.

did not want the hated symbol of tyranny to remain. Pieces of its stone were shaped into models of the building and turned into inkwells and other souvenirs. In time, there was nothing left of the despised prison.

The capture and destruction of the Bastille was a major symbol of the revolution. Every year thereafter, on the day the Bastille had been stormed and taken by the people of Paris, there were celebrations throughout France. To this day, July 14 is celebrated by French people everywhere, just as July 4 is celebrated by Americans. For French people, this marks the day when their freedom began.

Freed Citizens and a Captive King

When King Louis was told about the events at the Bastille the next day, he was stunned. "Is it a revolt?" he asked the friend who had brought him the unwelcome news. "No sire," came the response, "it's not a revolt; it's a revolution."[1] Frightened by the events of the previous day, King Louis and his military stepped down from their immediate plans to regain power. In a speech before the National Assembly, he told the delegates that the Royal troops had left Paris and that they would be safe. Just as importantly, he announced that he would call Necker to return and take his position as minister of finance again. The King was completely at the mercy of his people.

When news of what had happened in Paris reached the other cities and towns of France, many of them, too, exploded into revolt. Country homes and palaces of nobles were looted and burned. Forests and lakes that had been the private hunting and fishing places of nobles were taken over by peasants. Records of debts owed to nobles by peasants were destroyed.

Many nobles now suddenly realized that they could be in terrible danger. The peasants were boiling with rage, and there was nothing to control them. It would not be long before they began murdering nobles in revenge for the harsh treatment, the toil, the taxes, and everything else they had suffered for so long. So, many nobles began to leave the country, taking as much wealth with them as they could, to settle in foreign countries. These nobles became known as *émigrés*, a French word meaning people who leave their native country because they do not like it. One of the first of the émigrés was the king's own brother, the Comte d'Artois, who left France on July 16.

The National Assembly now had the problem of trying to calm the country down and end the violence that was flaring everywhere. The Third Estate delegates did not want to send soldiers out to restore order. That would make it seem as if they were attacking the very people they represented. But the delegates who belonged to a group known as the Breton Club, which included Maximilien Robespierre, came up with a solution. Even though some of these men were wealthy nobles, they almost all believed that drastic changes were needed to save the country. What they felt had to be done was for all the nobles to give up most of their privileges, which would mean the end of feudalism in France. That would take away the cause of the peasants' rage.

While the assembly was in session on the night of August 4, two Breton Club noblemen presented the club's plan. The hall was filled with spectators, mostly Third Estate commoners. The nobles in the assembly may have been fearful of their anger. At any rate, one after another, noblemen and Church officials stood up and agreed that their privileges, which were the cause of much of the country's trouble, *should*

On the evening of August 4, 1789, the National Assembly voted to abolish the privileges of all nobles. Now all French people would be considered as equal.

be abolished. A few nobles objected, but it did not matter. With growing excitement, the assembly made all taxes equal for everyone, ended tithing to the Church, abolished laws protecting game animals, and virtually made all the French people equal. By the end of the night, feudalism no longer existed in France.

The Citizens March

About three weeks later, on August 26, the assembly passed the Declaration of the Rights of Man and the Citizen. This spelled out all the freedoms that the commoners had gained and now shared with nobles and clergy. It was very much like the American Declaration of Independence and Bill of Rights. It provided the basis for a French government based on freedom of all people, under the law. This declaration had actually been written mostly by Lafayette, with the help of Thomas Jefferson, who was the American ambassador to France at this time.

Most of the country calmed down. But in Paris, where angry mobs had launched the revolution with the storming of the Bastille, there were suddenly new problems. Shipments of grain to the city were very late; bread was becoming scarce and expensive; and once more, many people were going hungry. As a result, angry crowds were again beginning to appear in the streets of Paris.

Another problem was that King Louis was obviously not at all pleased about the Declaration of the Rights of Man and the loss of most of the nobility's privileges. While he stated that he approved of the "spirit" in which they had been passed, he did not ever say that he accepted them. This was cause for suspicion to begin simmering in many people's minds.

Primary Source: From the Declaration of the Rights of Man and the Citizen, 1789

Articles:

1. Men are born and remain free and equal in rights. Social distinction may be founded only upon the general good.

2. The aim of all political association is the preservation of the natural and imprescriptible rights of man. These rights are liberty, property, security, and resistance to oppression.

3. The principle of sovereignty resides essentially in the nation. No body nor individual may exercise any authority which does not proceed directly from the nation.

4. Liberty consists in the freedom to do everything which injures no one else; hence the exercise of the natural rights of each man has no limits except those which assure to the other members of the society the enjoyment of the same rights. These limits can only be determined by law. . .[2]

Then, something happened that brought this suspicion to a boil. On October 2, the king and queen attended a banquet along with a number of nobles and army officers. Word leaked out that nobles had shouted out insults against the assembly. It was said that many nobles pinned on white ribbons, symbols of the king, and that someone had stamped on a red and blue ribbon, symbol of the revolution. To many people, this suggested that the nobles might be preparing to try to overthrow the revolution and restore the king to power. There was talk that the king should be forced to leave Versailles and come to Paris, where an eye could be kept on him.

Paris now had a new city government, made up of common people and called the *Commune*, or "Commons." On the morning of October 5, crowds of women from all parts of Paris stormed to the City Hall, where the Commune did its work, shrieking for bread. A few men began to join them. Before long, a mob of six thousand people, mainly women, was marching toward Versailles in the pouring rain to demand that the king return to Paris and lower the price of bread. Many of the women carried swords or pikes and some had muskets. A group of them were even pulling a cannon. On the way, they smashed windows and looted shops.

They arrived in Versailles about five o'clock in the afternoon. They went first to the palace but were unable to get in. The iron gates were locked, and soldiers of two of the foreign regiments were drawn up grimly behind them. Next, the women went to the hall where the National Assembly was at work. They literally invaded it, sitting down among the delegates and demanding to see the king. They wanted

Primary Source: A Woman's Testimony about the March on Versailles, 1789

Jeanne Dorothée Delaissement, age twenty-eight . . . stated that on last Monday, 5 October, in the morning, she, the declarant, was forced to go, as many other women were, with the crowd that wanted to go to Versailles. The women who dragged her in first led her to the Hôtel-de-Ville and then to Versailles. She saw nothing worth mentioning along the way. She knows that an individual whom she did not know at that time, but whom she came to know afterwards, named Maillard went to a great deal of trouble to keep order among the women, who were armed with pikes, sticks, pieces of iron, and other things, and that he succeeded in getting them to disarm en route. When they arrived at Versailles, a soldier dressed in a blue costume, who she learned was in the Regiment of Flanders, told her, in answer to her questions about people they should be suspicious of, that the Flanders Regiment would do them no harm, but that they must beware of the Royal Guards, who, during a meal, had trampled the national cockade.[3]

the king to lower the price of bread, they explained. It was Robespierre mainly who managed to calm them down.

A Captive King

Meanwhile, in Paris, thousands of soldiers of the National Guard were massing at the City Hall, also determined to march to Versailles. Lafayette got there on horseback as quickly as he could and tried to talk them out of it. It was no use. They wanted to get the king and bring him back to Paris. Lafayette finally gave up and agreed to lead them to Versailles.

In Versailles, the king agreed to see a few of the women. He listened to them, then announced that he would have all the bread in Versailles collected and given to them. Delighted, the women left. At eleven o'clock that night, Lafayette and the National Guard troops arrived. Lafayette sent a number of them to guard the palace. All seemed well.

But early the next morning, around five o'clock, another group of women got into the palace through a gate that had been left open. These were women known as fishwives, who sold fish in the marketplace in Paris. They lived hard lives, having to struggle to make a living. They had become tough, rude, and foul-mouthed as a result. They did not have much respect for anyone or anything, and they were not much afraid of anything. These women hated Marie Antoinette, whom they blamed for their problems. "Death to the Austrian," they shrieked, referring to the queen. ". . . tear out the heart of the *coquine* [Marie Antoinette], cut off her head, *fricasser* her liver and even then it would not be over."[4] One howled, "I'll have her kidneys in a fricassee!"[5]

Leaping out of bed, Marie Antoinette ran to the king's apartments with some of her ladies in waiting—women

The king's wife, Marie Antoinette, was unpopular with the commoners. They resented her lavish spending and her opposition to social reform.

who were part of her personal staff. There, they huddled behind locked doors with the king and the royal children.

Lafayette, sleeping in a nearby building, was aroused and rushed to the palace. Its courtyard was now swarming with people, but the National Guard troops were blocking the entrance into the palace. Lafayette hurried to the king's rooms and talked Louis and Marie Antoinette into stepping out onto a balcony with him so the crowd could see them. Expecting to be killed, they courageously did so. There were some yells of rage, but then Lafayette bowed and kissed the queen's hand. The crowd broke into cheers, and then began to yell, "À Paris [To Paris]!"[6]

"My children, you want me to follow you back to Paris," called the king. "All right, I will, but on condition that I will not be separated from my wife and my children."[7]

That afternoon, the king, queen, their children, and many courtiers rode to Paris in carriages, surrounded by the mob of fishwives and other women. The National Guard troops marched ahead, each man with a loaf of bread stuck on his musket's bayonet. Wagons full of wheat and flour trundled along in front of the procession. As they tramped through the mud of the rain-soaked road, the women chanted, "We won't lack for bread anymore! We've got the baker, the baker's wife, and the little apprentice!"[8] They seemed to believe that, as long as they had control over the king and his family, the problem of scarce bread was solved.

In Paris, the royal family was taken to a small palace, the Tuileries, where they would live, under guard, from then on. The king of France had virtually become a prisoner of the French people.

Political Disagreements and a Desperate Escape Attempt

The National Assembly was now the government of France. Assembly members went back to Paris with the King to get to work at trying to solve France's problems. The biggest problem that needed solving was that the government had almost no money and a lot of debts. In November, the National Assembly took a big step: It confiscated all of the land owned by the Catholic Church and put it on sale. This money went directly into France's coffers. But it was a controversial move and a lot of clergy disagreed with it. This was just the start of the movement in the revolution to take power away from the Church.

By the end of 1789, the delegates of the National Assembly had formed into a number of political groups with different ideas. Most of the groups set up places in various parts of Paris where they could meet to discuss their ideas and make plans. This was done in a formal way, with members standing up to give speeches in which they presented their ideas and suggestions.

One of these groups was the Breton Club, which renamed itself the Club of Friends of the Constitution. However, because its meeting place was in a building that had been a monastery of monks called Jacobins, it soon became known as the Jacobin Club. Maximilien Robespierre was still a member.

Since the National Assembly had been formed, Robespierre had often made speeches before it and taken part in all the debates and arguments about things the assembly wanted to do. He was not a very good public speaker. He had a grating, high-pitched voice and tended to use long-winded, complicated sentences. He had no flare for drama and no ability to use his voice to create excitement as speakers such as Mirabeau could. But when Robespierre made speeches about the problems of France, he spoke with such obvious sincerity about freedom and the rights of the people, that he held his listeners spellbound.

During the debates on the Declaration of the Rights of Man, Robespierre made several important speeches. In August, he spoke against any restrictions on what could be written in books or newspapers, saying that freedom of the press went hand-in-hand with freedom of speech. In December, he made a speech demanding equal rights for three groups of people who did not have them—Jews, Protestants, and actors, most of whom then were little more than vagabonds, without permanent homes. These people were all French citizens, Robespierre pointed out, and they deserved the rights that all other citizens had.

However, Robespierre did not convince many of the other delegates to adopt his opinions. He seemed too radical for most of them, too much in favor of tremendous changes that would make the country totally different. Most of the members of the assembly did not want to get rid of the king. They merely wanted to reduce his powers. But they sensed

Members of the Jacobin Club engage in debate. The group, of which Robespierre was a member, wanted France to become a republic rather than a monarchy.

that Robespierre actually wanted to end the rule of a king in France.

The Jacobin Club and the Cordeliers Club

Robespierre showed up at the Jacobin Club almost every evening and often gave speeches about his revolutionary ideas. The Marquis de Lafayette and some of his followers were also members of the club, but they did not share Robespierre's views. Still, Robespierre became a great favorite of most of the other members. In March 1790, they elected him the club's president. Under Robespierre's leadership, other Jacobin clubs, whose members shared the beliefs and ideas of the Paris club, were set up throughout most of France.

In April, Camille Desmoulins and a few others organized another club. It, too, had an old monastery as its meeting place. It was known as the Cordeliers Club, from the name of the area of Paris where the building was located.

The Cordeliers were fiery radical revolutionaries who wanted to do away with the king and turn France into a republic, like the United States. Among their members were two men regarded as the most violent revolutionaries in France, who believed the revolution would only succeed if all its enemies were wiped out. Jean Paul Marat, born in Switzerland, ran a newspaper called *The Friend of the People*, for which he wrote editorials that helped spread his ideas. Georges Jacques Danton was a successful lawyer in Paris and a skillful speaker who could excite people with his words.

Thus, from the beginning of 1790, it was clear that there were deep differences of opinion among the leaders of the revolution. The Cordeliers and some of the Jacobins

The Marquis de Lafayette served as a military officer in both the American and French Revolutions. He fought on the side of the colonists in the American Revolution and became close friends with George Washington and Thomas Jefferson.

wanted a republic. Mirabeau, Lafayette, and others wanted a constitutional monarchy—with Louis as king but ruling according to strict laws set down in a constitution. The followers of the Duke of Orleans also wanted a constitutional monarchy but with Orleans as king. And there were still nobles, lurking undercover, who wanted to restore France to the way it had been before the revolution began, with Louis as an all-powerful king and with all their privileges restored.

A shattering blow was struck against these nobles in June 1790. The National Assembly voted to abolish all nobility in France, making nobles the equals of everyone else. There were to be no more dukes, counts, or barons. From now on, everyone—from a former marquis to a ragged ditchdigger—would be addressed simply as "Citizen."

On July 12, the National Assembly passed an act designed to force the clergy into equality with the rest of the people. Known as the Civil Constitution of the Clergy, this act abolished all Catholic convents and monasteries and turned all members of the clergy into civil servants, paid by the government. It also ordered that bishops and archbishops be elected by vote instead of being appointed by the king.

The Royal Family's Plan

Some months later, the pope announced that he would not allow these changes, and that any priest or nun who accepted them would be excommunicated, or expelled from the Church. Of course, most French priests and bishops also refused to abide by the changes. In November, to try and force the clergy to accept the changes, the assembly passed a decree demanding that all clergy take an oath of loyalty to the constitution. More than half the clergy refused, and thousands of their parishioners backed them. On the other hand, many thousands of people began to demonstrate against the Catholic Church.

In the midst of all this, Mirabeau died on April 2, at the age of forty-three. It was said that his last words were that the monarchy was also going to die, and that many groups would fight for its remains. That seemed to be exactly what was happening. By the spring of 1791, France was again torn by disagreement and dissent.

Lafayette's group in the National Assembly was rushing to finish the writing of a constitution, in hopes that it would finally bring all the turmoil and violence to an end. But now, the nobles who wanted a return to the old ways struck a blow, with an attempt to help the king and his family escape from France.

On the night of June 21, Louis and his family, including his sister Elizabeth, entered a coach driven by a disguised nobleman and left Paris. The royal family members were disguised as servants. Louis was dressed in cheap commoner clothing. He carried identification papers that said he was a valet, a servant who takes care of a man's clothing and helps him make a good appearance. The queen was costumed as a governess, or "nanny," a woman who takes care of children. The thirteen-year-old princess and the six-year-old prince were both dressed in girls' clothing. The Comte de Provence and his wife, also disguised, were in another coach, but taking a different road.

Their plan was to go to the town of Montmedy on the border of the Austrian Netherlands (now Belgium) and cross the border to safety. It was their belief that Marie Antoinette's brother, Emperor Leopold, would eventually provide them with an Austrian Army. Louis would accompany that army

This engraving shows a disguised King Louis XVI and his family as they are confronted by revolutionaries during their escape attempt.

back into France in an invasion that, he hoped, would destroy the revolution and put him back in full power.

The Comte de Provence and his wife made it across the border. But for the royal family, things went wrong. In the morning, the coach was held up for hours by a broken wheel, and the soldiers who were supposed to have met the king to protect him did not arrive. Then, as the carriage passed through the town of St. Menehould late in the day, a man recognized the king from his picture on France's paper money. This man, Jean-Baptiste Drouet, was an ardent patriot who believed firmly in the revolution. He felt that, if the king were trying to sneak out of France in disguise, it could only be part of a plot to destroy what the revolution had accomplished.

Recapture and Disgrace

Drouet had once been a dragoon, a soldier of a cavalry regiment, so he was a skillful horseman. Flinging himself onto a horse, he galloped up a side road at breakneck speed to the next town, Varennes. There, he alerted the town officials that King Louis of France was going to try to pass through their town in an attempt to leave the country.

When the coach carrying Louis and his family reached Varennes, at about eleven-thirty that night, it was brought to a stop by a crowd of townspeople with torches and muskets, and a group of town officials. The officials were not quite sure what to do. They had only Drouet's word that the chubby man who said he was a valet was actually the king. Then, someone remembered that there was an elderly man living in the town who had lived in Versailles for many years and had often seen the king. Surely, he would be able to determine if the valet named Durand were really Louis XVI.

The man was sent for. When his eyes fell upon Louis, he automatically knelt, as commoners had always done in the presence of the king. Louis sighed. Realizing he could no longer hide his true identity, he said "I am indeed your King."[1]

Four days later, Louis and his family returned to Paris under guard, passing through crowds that shouted, "Long live the nation! Long live the National Assembly!"[2] Only a few weeks earlier, they would have been shouting, "Long live the king" at the sight of Louis. But now, whatever respect the king had left had been wiped out by his attempt to flee the country. Representatives of the National Assembly coldly told Louis he would no longer be regarded as king until he accepted the constitution.

Most of the members of the assembly still wanted France to be a constitutional monarchy, with a king. But outside the assembly, many people felt that the king should be tried and punished in some way for his attempt to leave France. And many more, especially the poorest working people, wanted the king to be removed and France to be a republic. Danton, Marat, and the rest of the Cordeliers Club did everything they could to make that idea spread. Robespierre and many of the Jacobins also began to speak loudly in favor of a republic. Slowly, the monarchists and the republicans began to regard each other as enemies.

On July 17, something happened that brought a confrontation between the two groups. At a park in Paris, members of the Cordeliers Club led by Camille Desmoulins set up a big meeting of people who wanted France to become a republic. Thousands attended, mostly working people.

Primary Source: Monsieur Drouet's Testimony, 1791

Gentlemen, my name is Jean-Baptiste Drouet, and I am the Posting-Master at Sainte-Menehould. . . On Tuesday the 2nd at half-past seven, after dinner, I saw two carriages in front of my door, namely a coach with six passengers and a cabriolet with two . . . In the coach there was a woman, whom I thought I recognized as the Queen, and on the seat in front of her to the left was a man. I was struck by the resemblance of his face to the likeness of the King printed on an assignat [paper money] which I had with me at the time. Since the morning a detachment of about fifty dragoons had been stationed at the Inn nearby. The officer in charge went up to the carriages and spoke in a low voice to the couriers accompanying them. . . They looked quite confused and kept repeating what they had said. My suspicions increased, but, being unwilling to cause a false alarm and having no one by me to consult, I let the carriages go. This I did most unwillingly. I was furious and ran about the place telling everyone that I believed the King was going away. I thought I had noticed that his face was pimply, but one of my uncles said I must have made a mistake. Perhaps I should have believed him if I had not seen the dragoons preparing to mount their horses. I then gave the alarm and made the drummer beat the call to arms. . . . [3]

Georges Jacques Danton was a powerful speaker and a leader in the early days of the Revolution.

During the meeting, two men were discovered in a hiding place, and people began to shout that they were monarchist spies. Enraged, the crowd hanged them.

The King Remains

Word of this quickly reached city hall. Fearing a riot, the mayor ordered Lafayette to take some National Guard troops to the park and break up the crowd. Upon reaching the park, Lafayette called out to the people to leave and go home. He was jeered and booed, and the crowd began to throw stones at the soldiers.

The soldiers opened fire. Fifty people went down, and the rest began to run. Lafayette may or may not have given the actual command to fire, but from this time on, Robespierre hated him. When Danton heard what had happened, he exclaimed, "If Lafayette has fired on the people, he's done for! Those who drink the people's blood die of it!"[4] Danton, too, became Lafayette's enemy.

The monarchists in control of the assembly now saw their chance to crush the republican movement. Under the pretense of preventing riots and lawlessness, they ordered the Cordeliers Club closed. Marat's newspaper and several others that supported the republican movement were shut down. An order went out for the arrest of Camille Desmoulins and others. All members of the Jacobin Club who were monarchists left the club, making it only about half as large as it had been. Despite this, Robespierre managed to hold the club together.

The republicans saw that they were in serious danger. Desmoulins and Marat went into hiding. Danton left France and went to England. Robespierre was convinced by a friend, Maurice Duplay, to leave the apartment where he was living and move secretly into Duplay's home.

Many of the monarchists who had left the Jacobin Club were members of the National Assembly. They, and others who believed as they did, formed a group that became known as the Feuillants. This, too, was a name that came from a religious order of monks.

The Feuillants now had control. In September, the constitution was finished as they wanted it. It preserved the monarchy and kept Louis as king, although with far less power than he had once had. It spelled out a great many things that he could no longer do. However, it did give him one important power—he could veto, or block, any law the assembly might try to pass that he did not like. On September 14, at a special ceremony, Louis swore to accept the constitution, and thus once more officially became king of the French people.

The National Assembly prepared to close itself down. Preparations began for the election of a new assembly that would govern France under the constitution. Most people believed that the revolution was now over.

They were wrong.

The End of the Monarchy

Now that the Feuillants held power in the National Assembly, they were able to pass legislation against the Jacobins and Cordeliers. Just before the National Assembly closed down, a popular and powerful Feuillant named Isaac Le Chapelier proposed the passage of a new law. This law would make trade unions and guilds illegal, as well as the right for workers to strike. Even more worrisome for the Jacobins and Cordeliers, he proposed that the government should control all political clubs. Le Chapelier thought that the Jacobins had too much power and had caused too much trouble. He suggested that any attempt by a club to criticize the government should be against the law.

Before Le Chapelier finished speaking, Robespierre stood up and challenged him. Robespierre charged that what Le Chapelier was suggesting would not only destroy the clubs but also do away with some of the basic rights that were in the constitution—freedom of speech, freedom of assembly, and freedom of the press. He declared that the revolution was not over as long as there were still people in France who wanted to return to the old ways of absolute monarchy. He showed how, with laws such as Le Chapelier was proposing, those enemies could gain strength and end liberty. Then, just as American patriot Patrick Henry had said, "Give me liberty, or give me death!" Robespierre exclaimed, "Let me perish myself before the death of liberty!"[1]

Thousands of spectators heard Robespierre's speech, and it made him a hero. Word of the speech swept through Paris. The next day, when the National Assembly came to an end, a huge crowd carried Robespierre triumphantly out of the hall on its shoulders.

Robespierre had become a tremendous favorite of the people. Both his supporters and those who disliked him agreed that he was an absolutely sincere and honest man. He could have become a millionaire by using his position in the government to do favors for people who would pay him for his help. Many politicians were doing this. But Robespierre utterly refused to do such things. He had become known as the Incorruptible, meaning a person who could not be bribed, or corrupted, for any amount.

There seems no doubt that Robespierre sincerely believed that a politician had to *be* incorruptible. He lived on nothing more than the salary he was given as a member of the assembly. He ate meager meals of bread, fruit, and coffee. Like most French people, he drank wine with his meals, but he watered it down a great deal. He did not have a girlfriend, and for amusement, he generally just went for walks in a park or sometimes went to a play. The only thing in which he seemed really interested was trying to make the revolution succeed.

Although he was not the most gifted speaker, Robespierre was able to move his listeners with his sincerity and intelligence.

Primary Source: Excerpt from the Le Chapelier Law, June 1791

Article 1. In that the abolition of any kind of citizen's guild in the same trade or of the same profession is one of the fundamental bases of the French Constitution, it is forbidden to reestablish them under any pretext or in any form whatsoever.

Article 2. Citizens of the same trade or profession, entrepreneurs, those who have set up shop, workers and journeymen of any skill may not, when assembled, appoint a president, secretaries, or trustees, keep accounts, pass decrees or resolutions, or draft regulations concerning their alleged common interests.[2]

The Girondins' Plot

On October 1, 1791, the newly elected government, known as the Legislative (lawmaking) Assembly, held its first meeting. The delegates were all men who had not been members of the National Assembly, because by law, those men could not serve two terms in a row. Of the new delegates, 136 were Jacobins, 264 were Feuillants, and 400 were not committed to any group.

The different groups began sitting together, each in a precise place, with the Feuillants on the right, the uncommitted delegates in the middle, and the Jacobins on the left. Thus, the idea of political positions was born. To this day, conservative politicians who do not believe in change are said to belong to the right, liberals who want great changes are said to be on the left, and moderates who do not side with either the right or left are said to be in the center.

One of the new delegates was Jacques Brissot. He led a small but very active group of delegates who were all members of the Jacobin Club. This group was known as the Girondins, because most of them came from a district of France known as the Gironde. The Girondins often met in the home of one of their members, Jean-Marie Roland, and his beautiful, intelligent wife, Madame Manon Roland. Working through her husband, Madame Roland actually gave the Girondins a lot of their ideas.

Like most Jacobins, the Girondins wanted to get rid of the king and make France a republic. Led by Brissot, they started a campaign designed to make the king—and the Feuillants—look bad.

They did this by forcing the king to use the veto against things that most people were in favor of. It was well-known that many of the émigré nobles were trying to talk some of the rulers of nearby countries into invading France, to help restore Louis to full power. So, on November 9, with the help of many of the uncommitted delegates, the Girondins managed to pass a decree ordering all émigrés to return to France. Of course, Louis could not allow such a decree to pass. Any émigré who returned would probably be executed or at least imprisoned. Two of the émigrés were the king's own brothers. He vetoed the decree.

Next, the Girondins managed to push through a decree that punished all Catholic priests who had not taken the oath to obey the constitution. It took away their pensions and forced them to leave the places where they were working.

Jacques Brissot was a leader of a group within the Jacobin Club that eventually gained a great deal of power.

Louis was a staunch Catholic. He was appalled by the decree, and vetoed it, too.

The Girondins Hope for War

As the Girondins had hoped, the king's popularity dropped sharply. Among the common working people he was called "Monsieur Veto."

A number of the uncommitted delegates of the assembly now joined the Girondins and Jacobins. The Feuillants were no longer the most powerful group in the assembly. By the end of 1791, the Girondins, also known as Brissotins, were in control. By March 1792, they were even able to force the king to dismiss the last of his noble ministers and appoint ministers who were favorable to the Girondins. Jean-Marie Roland became minister of the interior; Georges Jacques Danton became minister of justice; Charles François Dumouriez, a general, was named minister of foreign affairs. Part of Dumouriez's job was to get things ready in case of war, and this was important to the Girondins.

The Girondins wanted a war. They believed that the revolution was in grave danger from several foreign countries. In August 1791, the Austrian emperor and the king of Prussia (a small but powerful German kingdom) had issued a proclamation declaring that it was the duty of all European monarchs to help restore the king of France to his former power. In other words, they were urging the rulers of European nations to send armies to invade France, restore the king to full power, and destroy everything the revolution had accomplished. Accordingly, the Girondins believed that, instead of waiting to be attacked, France should attack first and declare war on Austria and Prussia.

The Girondins were not the only ones who wanted war. Lafayette and the Feuillants believed that a war could help them restore the idea of a constitutional monarchy. The king was also in favor of war, because he thought a war might restore him to full power. However, he pretended to believe as the Girondins did, that a war was necessary to protect France.

One of the few people who did not want war was Maximilien Robespierre. He was mainly against the idea of war because he saw clearly that it might help the king and destroy the revolution. He was also afraid that, during a war, it would be easy for some general, such as Lafayette, who had been put in charge of one of the armies, to seize power over France. The National Assembly had voted that its members could not serve in the new Legislative Assembly, so Robespierre could not speak there. But he could still argue his beliefs in the Jacobin Club, and he continued to do so. His main opponent was Brissot, and for more than two months, the two men spent many nights at the Jacobin Club, debating about the war.

Robespierre's Warning

Brissot believed a war would end the danger that foreign countries might invade France. He felt sure that French armies would be able to conquer their opponents. Robespierre was not sure of this at all. He was afraid that France was in no shape to go to war. It was still badly in need of money, food was still scarce, and the army was in bad condition. Most of the officers were gone. Six thousand of them had been nobles and had become émigrés. Most of the foreign regiments were also gone. France's new army was mainly made up of poorly equipped, untrained, and inexperienced men.

Brissot also seemed to believe that it was France's duty to try to bring the idea of the revolution to other countries. He felt that France's soldiers should be "armed missionaries," helping liberate the poor and peasants of other countries as the poor and peasants of France had been liberated. He spoke of the war as a "new crusade."[3]

Robespierre scoffed at this. He pointed out that no one liked people who tried to impose their ideas by force. The people the "armed missionaries" tried to convert would end up fighting them, Robespierre warned.[4]

In time, it became obvious that Robespierre had lost the debate. On April 20, 1792, the king went before the assembly and made a speech, announcing, "I have now come . . . to propose war—."[5] He received thunderous applause and cheers. Burning with excitement, the assembly voted to declare war on Austria, which was generally regarded as France's main enemy.

In those days, battles were fought by armies formed of groups of seven hundred to a thousand men, called battalions. They marched with machinelike precision and fired their muskets all at once, in volleys that hurled hundreds of bullets at the enemy in a single blast as deadly as a modern machine gun's. To fight in this fashion took training, discipline, and experience. In their first encounter with the well-disciplined, well-equipped Austrian battalions in the Austrian Netherlands (Belgium), the ragged, poorly trained, and inexperienced French troops simply turned and ran. Robespierre had been right.

The king soon found that he could not get along with his Girondin ministers. On June 10, he dismissed them all. He appointed a number of Feuillants to take their place.

As the war continued to go badly and as the money and food problems grew worse, the French people became angry and violent. Because the noblemen of the Second Estate wore a type of knee-length breeches known as *culottes*, most workingmen were now wearing long trousers, to show that they opposed the nobles. They had become known as *sans-culottes*, or "without breeches." Throughout the country, crowds of sans-culottes were rioting, setting fire to castles that had belonged to nobles, and even murdering people they suspected of being against the revolution.

Sans-Culottes Storm the Tuileries

On June 20, 1792, the people who had believed the revolution was over learned how wrong they were. At three o'clock in the afternoon, a mob of eight thousand sans-culottes of Paris, including women and children, stormed to the palace of the Tuileries. They intended to force the king to take back the ministers he had dismissed and stop using the veto. They were armed with clubs, axes, pikes, and a few muskets. A group of them was pulling a cannon along by ropes. The National Guard soldiers guarding the palace simply threw down their muskets and moved out of the way. The sans-culottes surged into the palace. It was a hot, muggy day. Most of them were dirty and they probably smelled. Many were drunk. They began to smash furniture and chop down doors with axes. There were shouts of "Down with the veto!"[6]

They broke into a small room and found Louis standing there, waiting for them. It was a brave thing to do, because he probably expected to be murdered. One man did lunge at him with a sword but was pulled back by others. Louis spoke to them with a great deal of dignity and courage, asking them what they wanted. To humiliate him, the sans-culottes made him put on a red stocking cap, a symbol of the revolution, and made him drink a toast to the success of the revolution. This seemed to calm them down. Then the mayor of Paris appeared and urged them to leave peaceably. After a time, they did, triumphantly slouching out of the palace, grinning and chuckling over their triumph.

Word of this trickled out of Paris and eventually reached the headquarters of the commander of the Prussian Army, the Duke of Brunswick. A nobleman, the duke was enraged to hear of such treatment of a king. In his anger, he did a rather foolish thing. In late July, he sent the people of Paris a message. He threatened to destroy the entire city if the king and royal family were harmed.

For the sans-culottes, this was nothing less than proof that the king was secretly communicating with the enemies of France. Stirred up by the writings of the fiery Marat in his newspaper *The Friend of the People*, a gigantic mob of twenty thousand sans-culottes marched to the Tuileries on the morning of August 10.

The royal family could hear a distant roaring sound growing ever louder, the noise of the approaching mob. The king and his family fled from the palace and sought protection from the Legislative Assembly. At the Tuileries, there was a battle between the mob and the Swiss Guard Regiment that was now guarding the palace and had sworn to protect the king. The soldiers were brutally wiped out— shot, stabbed, clubbed to death, hacked to pieces with axes. Several hundred sans-culottes also lost their lives.

The sans-culottes were French commoners who fought for social and economic equality. Their name refers to their refusal to wear knee-length breeches, or culottes, that were popular with the nobility.

The Beginning of Democracy

The assembly had Louis and his family put under guard in an old medieval castle known as the Temple Prison. They were under the supervision of the government of the city of Paris, the Commune. Many of the members of the Commune were men who had stormed the Bastille and attacked the Tuileries. They had no liking for the royal family.

Louis had been deposed—removed from power. He was no longer acknowledged as king. The monarchy was over. The revolution had been started by the bourgeoisie, the middle-class members of the National Assembly, most of whom wanted a constitutional monarchy. Now, it had been taken over by the sans-culottes, the working people and the poor, who wanted an end to kings. France was now to be a democracy, a government of the people.

The Death of Citizen Louis Capet

General Lafayette was concerned that the radicals were now in charge of the French government. Travelling to Paris, Lafayette delivered a speech to the Assembly and denounced the Jacobins. He was declared a traitor and a warrant was issued for his arrest. With the monarchy abolished, General Lafayette knew he was in danger. He escaped France for Belgium and surrendered to the invading Austrian and Prussian forces in August 1792 in order to save himself. With Lafayette a prisoner of the Austrians, General Dumouriez was appointed to take command of his army.

It was obvious that the National Assembly, which had been formed mainly to create a constitutional-monarchy type of government, was no longer of any use, since a constitutional monarchy was now impossible. A new constitution and a new government were needed. The assembly set up an election with which a new government could be formed.

On September 2, the important fortress city of Verdun was taken by the Prussians. Verdun was only one hundred fifty miles straight up the road from Paris. It was clear that

An engraving depicts the aftermath of the Battle of Verdun, where French forces were defeated by the Prussians led by the Duke of Brunswick. The image shows troops carrying the French commander, who committed suicide rather than surrender to the Prussian leader.

the Prussian forces were marching straight toward Paris, and everyone remembered the Duke of Brunswick's threat. Driven by fear and rage, mobs of sans-culottes stormed through Paris, murdering anyone they decided was an enemy of the revolution. They broke into all the prisons, where many people accused of working against the revolution had been sent—nobles, monarchists, priests who refused to sign the oath to the constitution. Most of these people, nearly fourteen hundred persons, were simply butchered, often in horrible ways. A man walking near one of the prisons while this was going on later wrote that the gutter leading from the building was actually flowing with blood![1]

Most of the working people of Paris were in favor of these massacres. They had been living in terror that the monarchists in the prisons might break out and start slaughtering *them*. Many of the Jacobins were also in favor of the massacres, believing they were cleansing France of those who were against the revolution. But the Girondins opposed the massacres, insisting they were a threat to law and order. A rift began to grow between the two groups. The Jacobins were clearly on the side of the sans-culottes and poor working people, but the Girondins had shown that they seemed to favor the wealthy, "upper-class" bourgeoisie.

On September 20, in an astounding victory, the French Army, led by Dumouriez, managed to halt the advance of the Prussian force moving toward Paris. The Prussian commander, the Duke of Brunswick, ordered a retreat all the way out of France. The threat against Paris was over.

One day later, the first meeting of the new government, the National Convention, began in Paris. Among the members were 110 Jacobins, including Robespierre, Marat, Danton, and Desmoulins. Around two hundred Girondins, including Brissot, had also been voted in. The rest of the 440 members were not committed to any particular point of view. Among the Girondins there was one foreigner—American Thomas Paine, who had been a tremendous force in the American Revolution. As a noted revolutionary, he had been granted French citizenship.

The King Is Put on Trial

The Jacobins sat at the left, in an area that happened to be higher than the rest of the hall. Because of this, they became known as the Mountain. Their leader, who planned most of what they did, was Robespierre.

The uncommitted delegates sat in a broad group in the center and were soon known as the Plain, and sometimes as the Swamp. The Girondins had now become the party of the right—"right-wing" conservatives. Their leader was still Brissot.

The first issue the National Convention took up was the kind of government France should now have. The decision was unanimous. The monarchy was abolished. No more kings! France was now a republic—a nation in which the government is a group of citizens elected to vote for what they feel the majority of the nation's citizens want. September 22 was announced as the first day of Year One of the Republic.

Almost at once, the Jacobins began demanding a trial for the former king. Some Jacobins wanted him executed as a traitor. On December 3, Robespierre stood up to speak. In a speech that became famous, he argued that a trial was not even necessary, because Louis had already been judged guilty by the *people*.[2] The people were the final judges, said Robespierre. He slyly asked a trick question—if the king were tried and found innocent despite the judgment of the people, would that not seem to mean that the people and the revolution were wrong? Such a possibility had to be prevented from happening. Robespierre urged that Louis simply be brought before the National Convention and sentenced to death.

Most of the Girondins did not want to see the king executed. Brissot made a speech in which he asked if it were really necessary for a man to die in order to end the monarchy.[3] Thomas Paine, the American, also argued against executing the king. He urged that Louis be sent to

America, to live out the rest of his life there.[4] The Girondins did everything they could to prevent a trial of the king.

But then, actual evidence was discovered that Louis had indeed been doing things to try to damage the revolution. A workman making repairs in the Tuileries had found a metal box hidden in a wall. It contained copies of many letters and documents, all signed by the king, revealing that he had been dealing with many people who were known to be against the revolution.

The discovery of the evidence ended opposition to a trial. In December, Louis was put on trial for treason. Because the first king of France had been a man named Hugh Capet, the former King Louis was now formally known as Citizen Louis Capet. He was allowed to select two lawyers to help defend him. For days, he was questioned by members of the National Convention.

The King Is Sentenced to Death

On January 15, 1793, the National Convention took a vote to determine whether Louis were guilty of conspiracy against the republic. All the deputies present voted yes.

The vote to decide Louis's punishment began at eight o'clock on the evening of January 16. Marat had demanded that each delegate should give his vote aloud, so that everyone could tell exactly where he stood. One by one, the delegates marched up to the platform. Some said only a single word, some made a few remarks. The convention hall was crowded with hundreds of spectators, who watched all this as if it were a play, drinking wine and brandy and eating oranges.

The voting came to an end at nine the next morning. There had been 321 votes for various kinds of imprisonment,

The king's family gather around him in farewell before he is taken to the guillotine.

but 394 for death. So, under majority rule, Louis had been sentenced to die. On Sunday, January 20, the National Convention set his execution for the next day. That night, he and his wife and children spent several hours together in a last tearful good-bye.

For hundreds of years, there had been two kinds of executions—one for commoners and one for nobles. Commoners were hanged—a slow, painful death by strangling. Nobles were beheaded with an axe—generally a quick, painless death. But now all Frenchmen were equal and were executed in the same way—by guillotine. This was a device named after National Assembly delegate Dr. Joseph Ignace Guillotin. It was a machine for quickly and efficiently cutting off a person's head. Guillotin had hoped that such a machine would be a humane, painless way to execute criminals.

At eight-thirty Monday morning, Louis was taken to the guillotine. It stood on a platform in the middle of an enormous open square known as the Place of the Revolution, just about in the center of Paris. (Today, this is known as the Place de la Concorde—the "Place of Harmony.") People sentenced to death by guillotine were generally taken to it in a horse-drawn wooden cart known as a tumbrel, but Louis went in a carriage, with cavalrymen riding in front and behind. When the carriage arrived, Louis stepped out and climbed the wooden stairs that led to the top of the platform and the guillotine. Twenty thousand people packed the square around the platform.

Citizen Louis Capet and the Guillotine

The executioners quickly and skillfully cut Louis's hair short, so that his neck was bare for the blade. Louis argued angrily for a moment when they started to tie his hands, then relaxed and let them do what they had to.

Louis tried to say some last words to the crowd, but the officer in charge of the soldiers quickly ordered the fifteen drummers to beat a steady roll that drowned out his voice. Those closest thought that the former king had declared he was innocent of the crimes he had been accused of, and that he hoped the shedding of his blood would not cause any misfortune for France.[5]

Then he knelt down and lay flat on the plank that was pushed forward so that his neck was directly below the blade. The executioner cut the cord.

Most accounts of the execution say simply that the blade plummeted down and the king's head fell. But one report states that Louis's neck was so very fat that Dr. Guillotin's painless and humane machine did not work properly. According to this account, the blade fell and the former king screamed, because his neck had not been cut through. It was said that a second try was needed, and this time it was successful.

When it was over, one of the guards picked up Louis's head and walked around the guillotine, holding the head high for everyone to see. There was a moment of silence, then the crowd began to give shouts of "Long live the republic!" A great deal of blood had spurted from the king's body and formed droplets and puddles around the bottom of the guillotine. People surged forward and began to dab this up with bits of cloth and paper and handkerchiefs. They wanted souvenirs of the historic event. After a time, the crowd began to break up and leave. There was much laughter and shouts of gaiety, as if the people were rejoicing.

Primary Source: Letter from Eyewitness Phillipe Pinel about Louis Capet's Execution, 1793

I doubt not that the King's death will be described in different ways, as the partisan spirit dictates, and that garbled versions of this great event will appear in the newspapers and be noised abroad in such a manner as to distort the truth. As an eyewitness . . . I am going to give you a faithful account of what happened . . .

When [Louis] arrived at his destination he looked at the scaffold without flinching. The executioner at once proceeded to perform the customary rite by cutting off the King's hair which he put in his pocket. Louis then walked up onto the scaffold. The air was filled with the roll of numerous drums, seemingly intended to prevent the people from demanding grace. The drumbeats were hushed for a moment by a gesture from Louis himself, but at a signal from the adjutant of the General of the National Guard, they recommenced with such force that Louis's voice was drowned and it was only possible to catch a few stray words like "I forgive my enemies."[6]

Some of them even joined hands and danced around the guillotine.

Marie Antoinette and her eldest surviving son were sitting at the breakfast table when the king died, but they were not eating. Suddenly, there was a boom of cannons in the distance. Through the window, they heard the soldiers on guard duty, shouting, "Long live the republic!" The queen and prince realized that Louis was dead, and they burst into tears.

Although with his infamous speech Maximilien Robespierre had probably done more than anyone to have the king executed, he was not among the crowd that watched the execution and celebrated afterward. He spent the day in his room in the Duplay house, and asked the Duplays to keep the window shutters closed all day. One of the young Duplay girls asked him why. He told her, "Because there is something that is going to take place today that it is not seemly that you should see."[7]

Citizen Louis Capet's body, with his head in a basket between his legs, was taken to a Paris cemetery. It was put into a cheap wooden coffin, which was covered with quicklime, a dissolving chemical, and buried ten feet deep. Years later, when the body was dug up for reburial, there was nothing left but an earthy sludge.

Civil War

The execution of the former king sent shockwaves throughout Europe. European monarchists were afraid that if something like that could happen in France, it could also happen in their own country. To show its disapproval, the British government forced the French ambassador to leave England. Hearing this news, the Girondin leader, Brissot, declared that France should declare war not only on Great Britain, but also on its allies. Soon, France was at war with six different European nations. In order to fight all of these enemies, France needed soldiers. So, on February 1, 1793, Brissot urged the National Convention to approve a national conscription. This meant that all men in France would be forced to serve in the army. Soon, three hundred thousand men were drafted into France's new army.

For a time, the French armies were victorious. French troops invaded Germany and captured the city of Frankfurt. Nice and Savoy, possessions of the Italian Kingdom of Sardinia, where Louis's sister was queen, were captured and made part of France. General Dumouriez's army advanced deep into Belgium.

Then, things suddenly turned around. Dumouriez was defeated by an Austrian army and had to fall back.

Primary Source: The National Assembly's Mobilization for War, July 1792

The National Assembly, after having heard the report of its Commission of Twelve, and having decreed the matter of urgency, decrees the following:

Article 1. When the internal or external security of the State is threatened, and the legislative body has deemed that extraordinary measures are absolutely required, it shall, by an act of the legislative body, declare as much and in these terms:

Citizens, the homeland is in danger!

Article 2. Immediately upon publishing that declaration, the departmental and district councils shall assemble, and, along with the town councils and communal councils, be on permanent watch. From this time forward, no public servant can leave, or stay away from, his post.

Article 3. All citizens capable of carrying arms, and having already served in the National Guard, will also be on active duty.[1]

He blamed this on the French government's inability to provide him with enough money, equipment, and trained soldiers. He issued a proclamation charging that the revolution had ruined France, and began making preparations to lead his army back to Paris. He intended to destroy the National Convention and set up a new monarchy. When he found that his soldiers would not stand for such an attempt to end the revolution, Dumouriez left his army and turned himself over to the Austrians, as Lafayette had done.

Dumouriez was, of course, condemned as a traitor by the convention. Because he had been on the Girondins' side for so long, the Jacobins began to accuse them of coddling traitors. A number of members of the Plain now joined the Jacobins, and the Girondins' power began to slip away.

General Charles François Dumouriez, whose arrest is shown here, was a celebrated military leader until his defeat at the hands of the Austrians at the Battle of the Neerwinden.

In March, in the region of France known as the Vendée, open rebellion broke out as the people refused to obey the conscription law. The Vendée peasants were mostly staunch Catholics and firm monarchists, and they would not be put into the army of a government that had killed their king and tried to destroy their religion. There were also similar uprisings in other places. Units of French soldiers were sent to put down these uprisings and found themselves fighting armies of peasants. Thus, there was now civil war in France—people of the same nation in armed conflict with each other.

To try to regain control, the National Convention set up a group of judges and lawyers called the Revolutionary Tribunal, to judge all activities against the revolution. The penalty for such activities was death. Several days later, on April 6, a nine-man group known as the Committee of Public Safety was also formed. It had control over the entire National Convention, deciding what laws should be made, raising and provisioning armies, and determining who would be arrested for treason. Most of the men picked for the committee were neither Jacobins nor Girondins, but one of them was Georges Danton.

The Girondins Are Arrested

A new small group of revolutionaries had appeared among the sans-culottes. Known as the Enraged Ones, they charged that there were men making money off the poor by holding back food to make the prices go up. Furthermore, they declared that these enemies of the people were being secretly protected by the Girondins. On March 9 and 10, groups of Enraged Ones made anti-Girondin demonstrations, smashing the presses of two Girondin newspapers.

Civil War

The Girondins quickly made a desperate move to try to regain their power and stop any more attacks on them. Marat, who was now president of the Jacobin Club, had been bitterly attacking them in his newspaper, so they launched an attempt to eliminate him. They accused him of being linked to the Enraged Ones, and of trying to destroy the revolution with "dangerous and radical" ideas. They urged that he should be brought to trial and expelled from the National Convention. With Marat out of the way, there would be less opposition to the Girondins' activities.

But their plan backfired. Marat was extremely popular among the sans-culottes of Paris, and huge crowds began to gather around the convention building, showing support for him. When Marat came to trial, he defended himself vigorously and was finally judged not guilty. The National Convention was invaded by sans-culottes, who carried Marat about triumphantly on their shoulders.

The Girondins did not give up. They demanded an investigation of the sans-culottes and the arrest of their leaders. They charged that the Convention was in danger from these people, and urged that it be moved from Paris, for its safety.

With the help of Robespierre, Marat, and the Jacobins, the Commune and the sans-culottes organized a major attack on the Girondins. On the morning of June 2, representatives of the Commune came to the National Convention and demanded the arrest of the Girondin leaders. The hall was packed with sans-culottes, and there was a tumult of shouts and threats in support of the demand. While Robespierre and the Jacobins of the Mountain silently and stolidly sat where they were, the badly frightened Girondins and the delegates of the Plain tried to leave the hall. However, they found the building surrounded by thousands of National Guard troops and sans-culottes, with dozens of cannons pointing toward the doors. The commander of the soldiers coldly demanded that the Girondins be arrested.

The delegates hurried back inside. Marat stood up among the Jacobins and asked to speak. He read off a list of the names of twenty-nine Girondins. Georges Couthon, a Jacobin who was one of Robespierre's strongest supporters, made a motion that these men be expelled from the National Convention. Giving in completely, the convention voted to accept the motion. Brissot and the other Girondin leaders were led from the hall, under arrest. The Girondins were through as a political force, and the Mountain and the Jacobins were now in complete control.

Marat Is Assassinated

In Normandy, a northern area of France, lived a twenty-five-year-old woman named Charlotte Corday. She believed that the ideas of the Girondins were the only hope for the success of the revolution, and that Marat and the Jacobins would destroy everything. In July, she left her home and went to Paris. She had only one reason for going there—she intended to kill Jean Paul Marat, in order to save the revolution.

At seven o'clock on the night of July 12, she made her way into Marat's house. She called out that she had special information for Marat, about traitors in Normandy. Hearing her, he called to his servant to let her in.

Corday entered the room where Marat was at work writing. Marat suffered from a horrible skin disease. At times, he could get relief from the itching and burning only by immersing his body in water mixed with vinegar and certain chemicals. He was seated in a high bathtub, with only his head, shoulders, and arms above the water. A board was placed across the top of the tub, on which he could do his writing. He and Corday talked for a while, then she began to give him a list of the supposed traitors. As he bent over to begin writing the names, the woman slid a knife out of her dress and stabbed him savagely in the chest. With blood pouring from his body, Marat yelled for help. Charlotte Corday did not attempt to run away,

Charlotte Corday was a Girondist who murdered revolutionary leader Jean Paul Marat. She was executed for her crime.

but simply walked calmly out of the room. Marat's servant leaped at the woman, knocking her to the floor and holding her there.

Marat's lung had been punctured, and he quickly died. When news of this swept through Paris, there was a tremendous surge of grief among the poor and working people. When time came for his burial, immense crowds followed the coffin through the streets. In Paris, several streets were renamed in his honor, and a number of towns throughout France were also renamed for him.

Charlotte Corday was tried in a court of law for murder and found guilty. On July 19, she went to the guillotine. Before putting her neck beneath the blade, she cried out, "I killed one man in order to save a hundred thousand!"[2]

Georges Danton had not been doing his job well, and on July 20, Danton and one of his friends were removed from the Committee of Public Safety. Two of Robespierre's friends, Louis de Saint-Just and Georges Couthon, were elected in their place. A week later, Robespierre was also placed on the committee. Danton left Paris to stay at his country home. With Marat dead and Danton gone, Robespierre was now the absolute leader of the Jacobins, and the most powerful man in France.

France's Victories

Robespierre was in charge of a dreadful situation. France was on the verge of collapse. A British army was beseiging the port of Dunkirk, a British-Spanish fleet was menacing the port of Toulon, and uprisings against the revolution were now widespread.

However, in August, an army officer named Lazare Carnot was elected to the Committee of Public Safety. Carnot turned out to be a military genius. At Carnot's urging, on August 23, Robespierre and the committee decreed that everyone in France was now part of the army. Unmarried men were to be soldiers, married men were to work at making weapons and ammunition, women were to sew uniforms and tents for the troops, and even children were to make bandages for the wounded.

This made it seem to most people as if they were all doing great and important work for their country and for the revolution. French armies became filled with enthusiastic young recruits who were wildly patriotic. Because they believed they were making war to defend their people's freedom, these men were willing to risk their lives in fierce attacks that enemy troops, who were fighting only for pay, could not stand up to. French generals had also invented a new way of warfare that helped even more. Instead of fighting in long lines, French battalions were formed into huge, dense rectangles that could smash into a Prussian or Austrian line and shatter it. Throughout September and October, French armies won resounding victories. The British were pushed back from Dunkirk, the Austrians and Prussians were pushed out of France, and the port of Toulon was regained. The rebellions in the Vendée and in Lyons were put to an end in brutal fashion, with thousands of people executed by firing squads, the guillotine, and even by drowning.

As French armies were beginning to win against the foreign enemies, it seemed to Robespierre and the Jacobins that all-out war also had to be waged against the enemies of the revolution in France. They felt that law and order could be restored within France only by a program of terror and violence aimed at people who did not make the revolution the foremost thing in their lives.

The revolution was Robespierre's whole life. Nothing else mattered to him. He believed that the revolution could turn France into a perfect nation, and he wanted to do everything in his power, whatever it might take, to help that happen. Historians point to letters Robespierre wrote before and at the beginning of the revolution, when he stood against violence and political executions. By 1793, however, Robespierre was more willing to resort to violence. In fact, with his homeland in danger, Robespierre resolved to do anything to protect it—even if it meant that thousands of people had to die.

So, in late summer of 1793, what was known as the Terror, or the Reign (rule) of Terror, began.

The Reign of Terror

On September 17, 1793, the convention passed the Law of Suspects. This law allowed anyone who seemed suspicious to be accused, arrested, and brought to trial by the revolutionary tribunals. "Suspicious" meant anyone who seemed like they were against, or even not working hard enough for, the revolution. With this law, many individual citizens lost their freedoms and had to prove their innocence. This began the Terror, where many innocent people lost their lives by guillotine.

One of the first sentenced by the law was the former queen, Marie Antoinette. She was accused of wasting enormous amounts of money, of persuading Louis to veto things, and of generally being an immoral person. None of these charges really deserved a death sentence, but they were regarded as proof that Marie Antoinette was against the revolution. She was sentenced to die. On October 14, she rode in the tumbrel with a number of others who had been sentenced to be executed on the same day. She appeared calm, and many people thought she seemed proud. When

Marie Antoinette was executed on October 14, 1793,
about nine months after her husband's beheading.

the executioner lifted her severed head, the watching crowd
broke into a roar of "Long live the republic!"

Soon after the former queen met her death, Brissot and
twenty leading Girondins were put on trial. They were
accused of seeking wealth and personal power. They were
all condemned to death. On October 31, they all went to
the guillotine together. Even one who managed to commit
suicide first was beheaded anyway. Eight days later, Madame
Roland was also executed. Her husband had escaped, but
when he learned of her death, he committed suicide.

As time went on, no one was safe. Men who had been
Third-Estate members of the National Assembly were

Primary Source: Edmund Burke on the Death of Marie Antoinette, 1793

It is now sixteen or seventeen years since I saw the queen of France, then the dauphiness, at Versailles; and surely never lighted on the orb, which she hardly seemed to touch, a more delightful vision. I saw her just above the horizon, decorating and cheering the elevated sphere she had just begun to move in, glittering like the morning star full of life and splendor and joy. O, what a revolution! and what a heart must I have, to contemplate without emotion that elevation and that fall! . . . little did I dream that I should have lived to see such disasters fallen upon her, in a nation of gallant men, in a nation of men of honor, and of cavaliers! I thought ten thousand swords must have leaped from their scabbards, to avenge even a look that threatened her with insult.[1]

guillotined. Generals who lost battles were guillotined. An elderly woman who had been a friend of King Louis's grandfather was guillotined. Even a number of sans-culottes and other common working people were guillotined. Robespierre didn't attend any of these executions and even told some friends that he regretted some of them, especially the execution of Marie Antoinette. While Robespierre instigated the Terror, it also seems that he was under growing pressure to crack down on enemies of the revolution by other members of the National Assembly.

The Terror was believed to be a way of keeping the revolution safe. But many Jacobins and most of the sans-culottes felt something else was needed. They believed that the Catholic religion had been nothing more than a way of keeping the peasants resigned to the rule of the king and the power of the nobles. Therefore, they decided that, to keep the revolution safe, it would be necessary to actually wipe out Christianity in France.

They began by totally changing the calendar. They did away with the seven-day week, replacing it with a ten-day period that had no Sunday. The months were also rearranged and given new names.

The Hébertists Rise and Fall from Power

The Enraged Ones now had a leader by the name of Jacques-René Hébert, who was one of the most wildly fanatic of all French revolutionaries. Hébert wanted the Terror to be increased, wanted the prices of food and other goods controlled by the government, wanted all property divided up and distributed evenly among the people. He was also one of those who wanted to eliminate Christianity in France. He led his followers in destructive attacks on some of the Catholic cathedrals of Paris, breaking things and holding mock religious ceremonies at the altars. There were similar attacks throughout France, with many churches ransacked and partially destroyed, and used for wild ceremonies that mocked Catholic rituals. Priests were forced to renounce their beliefs, forced to stop holding services, and even forced to get married.

Robespierre was not a Catholic and not really even a Christian. Still, he did not approve of this attempt to destroy

Primary Source:
The Law of Suspects, 1793

1. Immediately after the publication of the present decree, all suspects within the territory of the Republic and still at large, shall be placed in custody.

2. The following are deemed suspects:

   1—those who, by their conduct, associations, comments, or writings have shown themselves partisans of tyranny or federalism and enemies of liberty;

   2—those who are unable to justify, in the manner prescribed by the decree of 21 March, their means of existence and the performance of their civic duties;

   3—those to whom certificates of patriotism have been refused;

   4—civil servants suspended or dismissed from their positions by the National Convention or by its commissioners, and not reinstated, especially those who have been or are to be dismissed by virtue of the decree of 14 August;

   5—those former nobles, together with husbands, wives, fathers, mothers, sons or daughters, brothers or sisters, and agents of the *émigrés*, who have not constantly demonstrated their devotion to the Revolution;

   6—those who have emigrated between 1 July 1789, and the publication of the decree of 30 March (8 April 1792), even though they may have returned to France within the period established by said decree or prior thereto.[2]

Christianity. He spoke against it in the convention, arguing that it made France look bad to the other countries of Europe.

Danton returned to Paris in November and took his place at the convention. He began to speak out against the Terror. "Perhaps the Terror once served a useful purpose, but it should not hurt innocent people," he declared in one speech.[3] He also spoke against Hébert and his followers. Danton's friend, Camille Desmoulins, began to write articles in his newspaper, *The Old Cordelier*, condemning Hébert for being too extreme. Gradually, most of the members of the convention began to turn against the Hébertists.

On March 14, 1794, Hébert and the other Hébertist leaders were arrested and imprisoned. They were charged with planning to massacre the members of the convention and Jacobin Club in order to seize power and create a new government headed by Hébert and two others. It was also charged that they were being paid to do these things by agents of foreign governments. They were found guilty, and on Sunday, March 23, were all executed. Hébert was led to the guillotine, screaming in terror while the crowd laughed.

Now, Robespierre and Danton were the only two main leaders of the revolution left. Danton was immensely popular, but he did not have a clean record. There is considerable evidence that he probably took bribes during his time in government, even from the king.[4] To a person such as Robespierre, who was truly incorruptible, this would probably have made Danton seem like a traitor.

The Fall of Danton and Desmoulins

Some historians believe that Robespierre deliberately set out to destroy Danton. Others think he just reluctantly went along with his supporters. He made two speeches in which

Jacques-René Hébert was the editor of a radical newspaper, *Le Père Duchesne*. He called for increased violence against monarchists and the elimination of Christianity in France.

he seemed to be defending Danton, stating that Danton had always appeared to be a vigorous fighter for the revolution. Nevertheless, on the night of March 30, Robespierre and all but two members of the Committee of Public Safety signed a warrant for the arrest of Danton and his supporters, including Camille Desmoulins. They were charged with being secretly in favor of a monarchy and being guilty of corruption—taking bribes and making money by means of their position in government.

On April 2, they went to trial at the convention. Danton defended himself in wild, fiery speeches, but he knew that the convention would not dare go against Robespierre. He was right. Robespierre made a speech in which he argued that, even though Danton had been a great patriot, he should not be spared.[5] He reminded the convention that Brissot and Hébert had been great patriots, too, but had not been spared. The convention listened to him, then voted that Danton and the others were guilty and sentenced them to be executed.

The execution was set for April 5. As the tumbrel carrying Danton, Desmoulins, and others creaked past the Duplay house where Robespierre lived, Danton yelled out, "You will follow us, Robespierre!"[6]

Danton was the last of the group to be executed. When he stepped onto the platform, it was soaked with the blood of the others. In a loud voice that could be heard by everyone in the first few rows around the platform, Danton said to the executioner, "Don't forget to show my head to the people. It is well worth the trouble."[7]

Just as he had not gone to see the king's execution, neither did Robespierre go to see any of these other executions.

Robespierre was now the undisputed head of the government of the French Republic. He immediately began to work at trying to create a perfect republic. For him, this meant a republic in which all people were truly equal, and all were moral and virtuous—that is, law-abiding, decent, and without sin. He felt that only religion could make people moral and virtuous, and so he decided the republic needed religion. However, he did not want to try to depend on any form of Christianity, so he literally created a new religion, in which the god was known simply as the *Supreme Being*. This was a sort of mixture of Christianity, some of the ideas of the Enlightenment, and the spirit of the revolution.

Robespierre Is Arrested

On Sunday, June 8, Robespierre conducted a great celebration in honor of the Supreme Being. It was held in the same park where, a few years earlier, Lafayette's soldiers had fired into crowds of people. A miniature artificial mountain made of wood and plaster had been erected, at the top of which was an imposing statue. Dressed in a bright blue coat and wearing a crown of feathers on his head, Robespierre made a speech declaring that France was now showing the world that it believed in a Supreme Being and in immortality. There was an enormous crowd and there were hundreds of girls everywhere, throwing flowers. An orchestra played, people sang, and a number of cannons were fired in a salute. Robespierre appeared to be extremely happy, and most of the crowd enjoyed the spectacle. But many of the members of the convention, who had been ordered to be present, regarded all this as an example of Robespierre's growing desire to be in control of everything. Even many of the sans-culottes were upset. One revolutionary was even heard to mumble: "Look at the bugger. It is not enough for him to be master. He has to be God."[8]

Primary Source: Maximilien Robespierre on *The Supreme Being,* 1794

Frenchmen, you war against kings; you are therefore worthy to honor Divinity. Being of Beings, Author of Nature, the brutalized slave, the vile instrument of despotism, the perfidious and cruel aristocrat, outrages Thee by his very invocation of Thy name. But the defenders of liberty can give themselves up to Thee, and rest with confidence upon Thy paternal bosom. Being of Beings, we need not offer to Thee unjust prayers. Thou knowest Thy creatures, proceeding from Thy hands. Their needs do not escape Thy notice, more than their secret thoughts. Hatred of bad faith and tyranny burns in our hearts, with love of justice and fatherland. Our blood flows for the cause of humanity. Behold our prayer. Behold our sacrifices. Behold the worship we offer Thee.[9]

Robespierre began to lose his popularity. Many members of the convention believed he was trying to become dictator (single ruler) of France. Resistance against him and his methods began to grow, secretly.

On July 26, Robespierre made a speech defending himself before the convention. He began in a low voice that gradually rose to a shout as he went on. He let the convention know that he was aware a plot was being hatched against him. He hinted that he knew who the plotters were, and that they would be rooted out and executed.

That night, Robespierre's opponents met together and decided that they must defend themselves. The next morning at the convention, one after another, they stood up and made speeches condemning Robespierre as a would-be dictator and bloodthirsty tyrant. When Robespierre tried to speak, he was drowned out by shouts of "A bas le tyrant" (Down with the tyrant)![10] Robespierre either became enraged, astounded, or terrified. Whatever the cause, he simply could not speak. He could only make choking noises in his throat. Someone yelled out, sarcastically, "The blood of Danton chokes him."[11] Robespierre staggered to a chair and sat down, putting his head in his hands. He listened silently as the convention voted to have him and his followers arrested.

Robespierre Is Guillotined

They were taken to the city hall and confined in the room where the Committee of Public Safety worked. But everything was confused now, and the people of Paris began taking sides. The members of the Commune and the Jacobin Club declared that the convention had committed treason, and called for revolt. Other Parisians rushed to the convention hall, announcing their support for the convention.

Robespierre and his followers argued over what they should do, but could not come up with a good plan. Meanwhile, a horde of six thousand people, including many soldiers, headed for the city hall to seize the Robespierrists.

They broke into the building. Robespierre's brother, Augustin, who had come to Paris some months earlier, tried to escape through a window but fell to the street below and

This illustration depicts the French people carrying a representation of the Supreme Being. Robespierre fabricated a new religion that he hoped would take the place of traditional Christianity in France.

Robespierre lies wounded on a table after his arrest on July 27, 1794.

lay there badly injured. Louis de Saint-Just sat silent and motionless and let himself be captured. Couthon rushed to try to escape but fell down the stairs and suffered a head injury that knocked him unconscious.

No one knows exactly what happened to Maximilien Robespierre. One account says that he tried to shoot himself in the head, but only blew off part of his lower jaw. Another account says that a soldier shot him in the face. In either event, he remained alive with a shattered jaw, in terrible pain.

Robespierre was carried on a wooden board to a nearby room and put on a table. He lay there, semiconscious, for a long time. Eventually, a doctor arrived and bandaged his mangled jaw.

At five o'clock on the afternoon of July 28, 1794, Robespierre and twenty-two of his followers were taken in carts to the guillotine. The crowd there was the largest that had ever watched any execution. One by one, Robespierre's followers went under the blade.

Robespierre's eyes were closed, and he did not open them until he was carried up to the guillotine. He was placed in position. Either out of cruelty or because he felt it might interfere with the guillotine blade, the executioner bent over and tore the bandage from Robespierre's jaw. This must have been very painful, and Robespierre gave an agonized shriek.

It was the last sound he ever made.

Legacy of the French Revolution

Since Maximilien Robespierre's death over two hundred years ago, he has remained a controversial figure. Many historians have regarded Robespierre as the most violent figure in the French Revolution, the man who was ultimately responsible for the Terror. However, other historians have argued that we do not, in fact, know Robespierre's role in the executions of leaders such as Danton and others. These historians state that Robespierre often fought against the most radical revolutionaries and was accused of being moderate by others in his party. What we do know is that Robespierre believed in the French Revolution so much that he would do almost anything to protect it. Today, while there are many schools and streets named after Robespierre in France, there is no memorial for him in Paris. In fact, Robespierre is one of the only major revolutionaries who does not hold a place of honor in Paris, even though everyone would agree that he was the most important person in the French Revolution.

Following Robespierre's death, the Terror came to an end. The convention continued to govern, but slowly its power seeped away. There were several attempts by former nobles to seize control and turn France into a kingdom again, but they failed. However, there was a growing feeling against the power that working people had, and gradually the sans-culottes, the Jacobins, and other groups faded away.

On November 9, 1799, the popular and successful General Napoleon Bonaparte seized control of the government. He made himself dictator of France. With that, the revolution was over.

In the seventy-seven years following Robespierre's death, France had many kinds of government—once a dictatorship, twice a kingdom again, once more a republic, and two times an empire. In 1870, it became a republic again, and has remained one. But whatever the kind of government, the basic changes the revolution brought about were never lost. There were never again any restrictions based on class. The son of an ordinary farmer could become commander of the French Army, a cardinal of the Catholic Church, or the highest official of the government. Anyone willing to work hard could become wealthy and respected. Anyone could own property. There was freedom of religion, and generally, freedom of the press.

The French Revolution's effect has lasted to this day. French armies brought revolutionary ideas into other European countries. Some of those countries eventually had revolutions of their own. Nations that had long been ruled by nobles became republics and democracies, ruled by all the people.

The ideas of Robespierre, Danton, and others inspired new political ideas. Before the revolution, no country had any kind of government program for helping poor people. Robespierre and the Jacobins believed it was a government's duty to help. Today, many nations have government aid for the poor, and pensions and medical help for elderly people, which have their roots in the French Revolution.

Some of the ideas of the French Revolution inspired the twentieth-century political system called Communism. This is a system based on the idea that all people should be absolutely equal in every way. The Russian Revolution of 1917 was much like the French Revolution. Ideas that were formed during the French Revolution inspired Russia's communist government for some seventy-five years. In Russia's capital city, Robespierre was hailed as a hero and a statue of him was erected. While Russia's Communist government eventually fell, the People's Republic of China still regards itself as a Communist nation today.

Primary Source: Letter from Alexander Hamilton on the French Revolution, 1794

If there be anything solid in virtue—the time must come when it will have been a disgrace to have advocated the Revolution of France in its late stages . . . The French Revolution is a political convulsion that in a great or less degree shakes the whole civilized world and it is of real consequence to the principles and of course to the happiness of a Nation to estimate it rightly.[1]

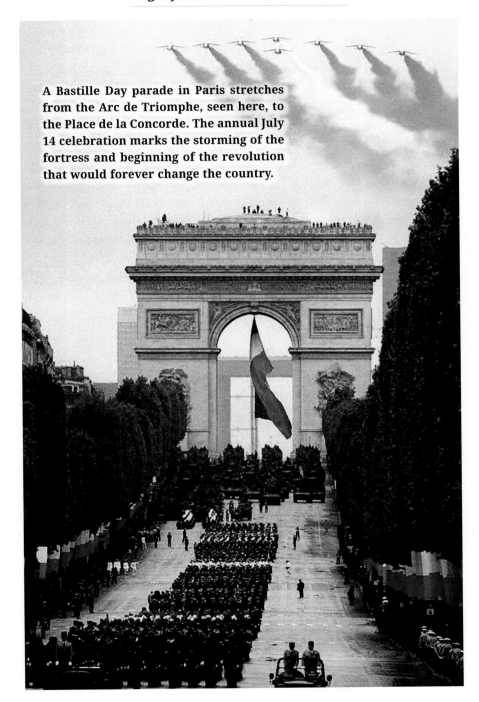

A Bastille Day parade in Paris stretches from the Arc de Triomphe, seen here, to the Place de la Concorde. The annual July 14 celebration marks the storming of the fortress and beginning of the revolution that would forever change the country.

Many people see the French Revolution as a terrible event because of its violence and bloodshed. But like the American Revolution, it showed that common people could rise up and fight to gain freedom. The main idea of the French and American revolutions—that a nation's government should be in the hands of all its people—became widespread. These ideas are the basis for most governments in the world today.

While the Reign of Terror was a dark period in history, the French Revolution began with peoples' desire to be fairly represented by their government. It achieved its goal. Today, France is a republic whose laws are still based on the Declaration of the Rights of Man and of the Citizen. The French flag is the tricolor—red, white, and blue—that represents the colors of the revolution. France's national anthem is "La Marseillaise," a battle hymn written by a revolutionary soldier. And France's renowned national motto, "Liberté, Egalité, Fraternité," symbolizing every citizen's right to liberty, equality, and fraternity, was coined by none other than Maximilien Robespierre.

1789—May 5: The Estates-General meets in Versailles.

June 7: The Third Estate votes to name itself the National Assembly.

June 20: The National Assembly delegates take the Tennis Court Oath.

June 23: The king orders the three estates to leave the meeting hall; the National Assembly refuses.

July 14: The Bastille is captured by a Paris mob.

Late July–Early August: Peasant revolts take place throughout France.

August 4: Feudalism ends in France.

August 26: The National Assembly produces the Declaration of the Rights of Man and the Citizen.

October 5: Six thousand women of Paris march to Versailles to demand bread.

October 6: The king and royal family are taken to Paris.

1790—June 19: Nobility is abolished.

July 12: The National Assembly decrees the Civil Constitution of the Clergy.

1791—June 21: The king and royal family attempt to escape from the country.

September 14: Louis accepts the constitution; France becomes a constitutional monarchy.

October 1: The Legislative Assembly meets as the new government of France.

1792—April 20: Declaration of war against Austria.

June 10: The king dismisses the Girondin ministers.

June 20: The Parisian sans-culottes invade the Tuileries.

Late July: The Prussian commander issues a threat against the city of Paris.

August 10: The sans-culottes invade the Tuileries and force the king to flee to the assembly for safety; the king is deposed.

August 13: The royal family is imprisoned in the Temple Prison.

September 2: The fortress of Verdun is captured by the Prussians; Prison massacres take place in Paris.

September 20: A French army defeats the Prussians.

September 21: The National Convention holds its first meeting.

September 21–22: The monarchy is abolished; France becomes a republic.

December: The trial of the king begins.

1793—**January 17:** The king is condemned to death.

January 21: The king is executed.

February 1: War is declared against Great Britain and the Dutch Republic.

March: Civil war begins in the Vendée; the Revolutionary Tribunal is created.

April 6: The Committee of Public Safety is created.

June 2: The Girondins are expelled from the convention and placed under house arrest.

July 27: Robespierre is appointed to the Committee of Public Safety; the Reign of Terror begins.

October 31: The Girondin leaders are executed.

1794—**March 14:** The Hébertist leaders are arrested.

March 23: The Hébertist leaders are executed.

March 30: Danton, Desmoulins, and other Dantonists are arrested.

April 5: The Dantonists are executed.

June 8: The Festival of the Supreme Being is held in Paris.

July 27: Robespierre and his supporters are arrested.

July 28: Robespierre and his supporters are executed; the Reign of Terror ends.

1799—Napoleon Bonaparte takes control of the government, making himself the dictator of France.

CHAPTER NOTES

CHAPTER 1.   The Guillotine

1. John Gideon Millingen, *Recollections of Republican France, from 1790-1801* (London: H. Colburn, 1848), pp. 204–206.

CHAPTER 2.   L'Ancien Régime

1. Arthur Young, "Travels During the Years 1787, 1788, and 1789," *Library of Economics and Liberty,* http://www.econlib.org/library/YPDBooks/Young/yngTF5.html (accessed July 2, 2015).
2. "Jean-Jacques Rousseau on the Social Contract (1762)," *Alpha History: The French Revolution,* Alpha History, http://alphahistory.com/frenchrevolution/rousseau-social-contract-1762/ (accessed August 16, 2015).
3. Simon Schama, *Citizens: A Chronicle of the French Revolution* (New York: Alfred A. Knopf, 1989), p. 328.

CHAPTER 3.   Revolutionary Rumblings

1. Hanover College Department of History, "Cahier of 1789, The Third Estate of Versailles," *Hanover Historical Texts Project,* last modified March 2001, http://history.hanover.edu/texts/cahiers3.html.
2. "The Oath of the Tennis Court," *The History Guide,* last revised May 13, 2004, http://www.historyguide.org/intellect/tennis_oath.html.

CHAPTER 4.   The Storming of the Bastille

1. Simon Schama, *Citizens: A Chronicle of the French Revolution* (New York: Alfred A. Knopf, 1989), p. 363.
2. J.M. Thompson, *The French Revolution* (Oxford, England: Basil Blackwell, 1964), p. 24.
3. Olivier Bernier, *Words of Fire, Deeds of Blood: The Mob, the Monarchy, and the French Revolution* (Boston: Little, Brown and Company, 1989), p. 17.
4. Jules Michelet, *History of the French Revolution* (Chicago: University of Chicago Press, 1967), p. 150.
5. Schama, p. 382.
6. Ibid.
7. Jack R. Censer and Lynn Hunt, "Desmoulins on His Own Role," Liberty, Equality, Fraternity: Exploring the French Revolution, *The Roy Rosenzweig Center for History and New Media and the American Social History Project,* https://chnm.gmu.edu/revolution/d/380/ (accessed July 1, 2015).

CHAPTER 5. Freed Citizens and a Captive King

1. Evelyne Lever, *Louis XVI,* (Paris: Fayard, 1985), p. 512.
2. William C. Fray and Lisa A. Spar, "Declaration of the Rights of Man—1789," *The Avalon Project,* 1996, http://avalon.law.yale.edu/18th_century/rightsof.asp (accessed July 1, 2015).
3. Jack R. Censer and Lynn Hunt, "Women Testify Concerning Their Participation in the October Days," Liberty, Equality, Fraternity: Exploring the French Revolution, *The Roy Rosenzweig Center for History and New Media and the American Social History Project,* https://chnm.gmu.edu/revolution/d/474/ (accessed July 1, 2015).
4. Simon Schama, *Citizens: A Chronicle of the French Revolution* (New York: Alfred A. Knopf, 1989), p. 467.
5. Christopher Hibbert, *The Days of the French Revolution* (New York: William Morrow and Company, Inc., 1980), p. 101.
6. M.J. Sydenham, *The French Revolution* (New York: G.P. Putnam's Sons, 1965), p. 61.
7. Olivier Bernier, *Words of Fire, Deeds of Blood: The Mob, the Monarchy, and the French Revolution* (Boston: Little, Brown and Company, 1989), p. 72.
8. Ibid., p. 73.

CHAPTER 6. Political Disagreements and a Desperate Escape Attempt

1. Simon Schama, *Citizens: A Chronicle of the French Revolution* (New York: Alfred A. Knopf, 1989), p. 554.
2. Olivier Bernier, *Words of Fire, Deeds of Blood: The Mob, the Monarchy, and the French Revolution* (Boston: Little Brown and Company, 1989), p. 279.
3. Jack R. Censer and Lynn Hunt, "The Flight to Varennes," Liberty, Equality, Fraternity: Exploring the French Revolution, *The Roy Rosenzweig Center for History and New Media and the American Social History Project,* https://chnm.gmu.edu/revolution/d/313/ (accessed July 2, 2015).
4. Frank Dwyer, *Danton* (New York: Chelsea House Publishers, 1987), p. 61.

CHAPTER 7. The End of the Monarchy

1. Simon Schama, *Citizens: A Chronicle of the French Revolution* (New York: Alfred A. Knopf, 1989), p. 580.
2. Jack R. Censer and Lynn Hunt, "Le Chapelier Law," Liberty, Equality, Fraternity: Exploring the French Revolution, *The Roy Rosenzweig Center for History and New Media and the American Social History Project,* https://chnm.gmu.edu/revolution/d/370/ (accessed July 2, 2015).

3. J.M. Thompson, *The French Revolution* (Oxford, England: Basil Blackwell, 1964), p. 256.
4. David P. Jordan, *The Revolutionary Career of Maximilien Robespierre* (New York: The Free Press, 1985), p. 86.
5. Christopher Hibbert, *The Days of the French Revolution* (New York: William Morrow and Company, Inc., 1980), p. 101.
6. Olivier Bernier, *Words of Fire, Deeds of Blood: The Mob, the Monarchy, and the French Revolution* (Boston: Little, Brown and Company, 1989), p. 6.

CHAPTER 8.   The Death of Citizen Louis Capet

1. Christopher Hibbert, *The Days of the French Revolution* (New York: William Morrow and Company, 1980), p. 177.
2. Olivier Bernier, *Words of Fire, Deeds of Blood: The Mob, the Monarchy, and the French Revolution* (Boston: Little, Brown and Company, 1989), p. 391.
3. Hibbert, p. 184.
4. Simon Schama, *Citizens: A Chronicle of the French Revolution* (New York: Alfred A. Knopf, 1989), p. 665.
5. Ibid., p. 669.
6. Jack R. Censer and Lynn Hunt, "Execution of the King," Liberty, Equality, Fraternity: Exploring the French Revolution, *The Roy Rosenzweig Center for History and New Media and the American Social History Project,* https://chnm.gmu.edu/revolution/d/327/ (accessed July 2, 2015).
7. Hibbert, p. 211.

CHAPTER 9.   Civil War

1. Jack R. Censer and Lynn Hunt, "Mobilization for War," Liberty, Equality, Fraternity: Exploring the French Revolution, *The Roy Rosenzweig Center for History and New Media and the American Social History Project,* https://chnm.gmu.edu/revolution/d/424/ (accessed July 2, 2015).
2. David L. Dowd, *The French Revolution* (New York: American Heritage, 1965), p. 118.

CHAPTER 10.   The Reign of Terror

1. Paul Halsall, "Edmund Burke: The Death of Marie Antoinette," *Modern History Sourcebook,* August 1997, http://www.fordham.edu/halsall/mod/1793burke.html.

2. Jack R. Censer and Lynn Hunt, "The Law of Suspects," Liberty, Equality, Fraternity: Exploring the French Revolution, *The Roy Rosenzweig Center for History and New Media and the American Social History Project,* https://chnm.gmu.edu/revolution/d/417/ (accessed July 2, 2015).
3. Susan Banfield, *The Rights of Man, the Reign of Terror: The Story of the French Revolution* (New York: J.B. Lippincott, 1989), p. 162.
4. David P. Jordan, *The Revolutionary Career of Maximilien Robespierre* (New York: The Free Press, 1985), p. 247.
5. Christopher Hibbert, *The Days of the French Revolution* (New York: William Morrow and Company, Inc., 1980), p. 239.
6. Ibid., p. 248.
7. Simon Schama, *Citizens: A Chronicle of the French Revolution* (New York: Alfred A. Knopf, 1989), p. 820.
8. Peter McPhee, *Robespierre: A Revolutionary Life* (New Haven, CT: Yale University Press, 2012), p. 198.
9. Paul Halsall, "Maximilien Robespierre: The Cult of the Supreme Being," *Modern History Sourcebook,* August 1997, http://www.fordham.edu/halsall/mod/robespierre-supreme.html.
10. J. M. Thompson, *The French Revolution* (Oxford, England: Basil Blackwell, 1964), p. 514.
11. Schama, p. 844.

CHAPTER 11. Legacy of the French Revolution

1. Jack R. Censer and Lynn Hunt, "Alexander Hamilton on the French Revolution," Liberty, Equality, Fraternity: Exploring the French Revolution, *The Roy Rosenzweig Center for History and New Media and the American Social History Project,* https://chnm.gmu.edu/revolution/d/593/ (accessed July 2, 2015).

GLOSSARY

ancien régime—The name for the French government before the French Revolution, when French society was divided into three estates: the First Estate (clergy), the Second Estate (nobles), and the Third Estate (commoners).

Bastille—French prison that was stormed by an angry mob at the beginning of the French Revolution in 1789.

bourgeoisie—Those who belonged to what would be known today as the French "middle class."

Breton Club—An early political club, with Robespierre as a member, that would later become known as the Jacobin Club.

constitutional monarchy—A form of government where the king or queen's powers are restricted by a constitution and a legislative body.

Cordeliers Club—A radical political club, with Jean Paul Marat, Camille Desmoulins, and Georges Jacques Danton as members, that wanted to do away with the king and turn France into a republic.

Estates-General—The legislative body of France until 1789.

feudalism—A social system used in France until the Revolution, whereby the nobility was given land by the King, which was then worked by peasants in return for military protection.

Feuillants—A group of moderate revolutionaries who wanted France's government to become a constitutional monarchy.

Girondins—A group of Jacobins, led by Jacques Brissot, who tended to support the wealthier bourgeoisie, rather than the interests of the working people.

guillotine—A machine used for executions by beheading during the Reign of Terror.

Hébertists—Also known as the Enraged Ones and led by Jacques-René Hébert, this group was the most fanatical of all the French revolutionists.

Jacobin Club—The most famous political group of the French Revolution, led by Maximilien Robespierre.

monarchist—Someone who supports the king and the monarchy.

sans-culottes—Literally meaning "without breeches," the name for French commoners and working-class people during the Revolution.

Further Reading

Conner, Clifford D. *Jean Paul Marat: Tribune of the French Revolution.* London: Pluto Press, 2012.

Gregory, Josh. *The French Revolution.* New York: Scholastic, 2013.

Jolkovski, Emily Kay. *The Incorruptible: Maximilien Robespierre and the Terror.* Smirking Rat Productions, 2013.

LaMonica, Michael J. and Tom Motley. *French Revolutions for Beginners.* Danbury, CT: For Beginners, 2014.

McPhee, Peter. *Robespierre: A Revolutionary Life.* New Haven, CT: Yale University Press, 2012.

Websites

History.com: French Revolution
www.history.com/topics/french-revolution
Features articles and videos on topics related to the French Revolution.

HistoryToday: Robespierre and the Terror
www.historytoday.com/marisa-linton/robespierre-and-terror
Provides a detailed biography of Robespierre and his role in the Reign of Terror.

INDEX

A

American Declaration of Independence, 48

American Revolution, 9, 30, 83, 118

Antoinette, Marie, 21, 23, 52, 54, 61, 63, 90, 100–102

d'Artois, Comte, 23, 46

B

Bastille, 35–39, 41–44, 45, 48, 80

Bonaparte, Napoleon, 115

bourgeoisie, 11–12, 15–16, 80, 83

Breteuil, Baron de, 38

Breton Club, 46, 48, 55–56. *See also* Jacobin Club

Brissot, Jacques, 72, 74–76, 83–84, 91, 96, 101, 107

Brissotins. *See* Brissot, Jacques; Girodins

Brunswick, Duke of, 78, 82–83

C

Capet, Louis Citizen. *See* Louis XVI, king of France

Carnot, Lazare, 98

Catholic Church, 9, 11, 55, 60–61, 72, 74, 94, 103, 105, 115

Civil Constitution of the Clergy, 60

Committee of Public Safety, 94, 98, 107, 110

Commune, 50, 80, 95, 110

Communism, 116

constitutional monarchy, 60, 64, 75, 80, 81

Corday, Charlotte, 96–97

Cordeliers Club, 58, 60, 64, 66–68

Couthon, Georges, 96, 98, 113

D

Danton, Georges Jacques, 58, 64, 66–67, 74, 83, 94, 98, 105, 107, 110, 114–115

Declaration of the Rights of Man and the Citizen, 48–49, 56, 118

Delaissement, Jeanne Dorothée, 51

Desmoulins, Camille, 38–39, 41, 58, 64, 66–67, 83, 105, 107–108

Drouet, Jean-Baptiste, 63, 65

Dumouriez, Charles François, 74, 81, 83, 91, 93

Duplay, Maurice, 67, 90, 107

E

Enlightenment, 15–20, 108

Enraged Ones, 94–95, 103

Estate System, 9, 11–12, 14–20

Estates-General, 24–27, 30–31, 37–38

F

feudalism, 9, 12, 14–15, 46, 48

Feuillants, 67, 68, 71–72, 74–75, 77

fishwives, 52, 54

Flanders Regiment, 51

French Revolution

  abolition of nobility, 35, 48, 60

  climate before revolution, 9, 11–12, 14–20, 21, 23–27, 29–31, 33–34

  Estates-General, 24, 26–27, 30–31, 37–38

  legacy, 114–116, 118

  Louis executed, 81–85, 87–90

  Reign of Terror, 99, 100–105, 107–110, 114

  rise of Napoleon, 115

  storming of the Bastille, 35–39, 41–44, 45, 48, 80

G

Girondins, 71–72, 74–75, 77, 83–85, 91, 93–96, 101

Guillotin, Joseph Ignace, 87–88

guillotine, 5–8, 87–88, 90, 97, 99–102, 105, 110, 113

H

Hamilton, Alexander, 116

Hébert, Jacques-René, 103, 105, 107

Henry, Patrick, 69

I

Invalides, 42

J

Jacobin Club, 56, 58, 60, 64, 67, 68, 71–72, 75, 81, 83–84, 93–96, 98–99, 103–105, 110, 115–116. *See also* Breton Club

Jefferson, Thomas, 48

Jews, 11, 56